Infants

Infants
Robert B. McCall

Harvard University Press
Cambridge, Massachusetts
London, England
1979

Copyright © 1979 by The McCall Children's Trust
All rights reserved
Printed in the United States of America

Library of Congress Cataloging in Publication Data

McCall, Robert B   1940–
  Infants.

  Includes index.
  1. Infant psychology. 2. Children—Management.
I. Title.
BF723.I6M275   155.4'22   79-14784
ISBN 0-674-45265-8

To

Blanche and Emma
my older teachers

Darin and Stacey
my younger teachers

Rozanne
my fellow student

Preface

THE BIRTH OF a child is a momentous event. Not only is it the beginning of a new person, but it brings new joys, frustrations, and responsibilities to adults now transformed into parents.

These new responsibilities start almost immediately. Shall the infant be breast- or bottle-fed? That decision may depend on the mother's feelings about herself, her need to work, her husband's desire to take an active role in childcare, their concerns about nutrition and natural immunizations, and so forth. Life quickly becomes complicated.

Decisions about method of feeding, scheduling, who takes the 2 a.m. session, and what kind of diapers to use are only the beginning. Beyond their immediate physical needs babies have personalities, and parents want to get to know them. But infants are not like adults. For one thing, they don't talk. How do you get acquainted with a newborn? What do they see and hear? Are those occasional smiles gas pains or hellos? How actually do you love a baby? Loving another person, even a baby, is more than cuddling and kissing: these are expressions of love, not love itself.

And babies cry—some of them interminably. An infant's cry is one of the most irritating sounds imaginable. Perhaps nature has made it so. But what do you do when the crying persists even after the baby has been fed, changed, and checked for open pins? Some new parents become totally frustrated because they want to calm their newborn infants but nothing seems to work. Picking them up all the time might spoil them (it doesn't), but you can't leave them in the crib screeching either. Crying is normal, and a baby who never cries may have a greater problem than one who cries several hours a day.

Beyond the bread-and-butter problems of how to feed and bathe and comfort an infant, there is the question of how to stimulate a baby during those important first years of life. All parents want their child to be mentally competent and to be able to function well in society. Much has been written about the importance of the early years of life in shaping a child's intelligence and personality. Many parents are concerned that they are not doing enough. They feel guilty, but they don't know what to do.

The birth of a new baby, however personally joyful, is a financial burden. Husbands think about moonlighting, and wives are torn between their responsibility as a mother and their need to contribute to the family finances or their desire for a career. For many women there is no choice—the wife's income is not supplementary, it's absolutely necessary. But what will happen to the infant's development if both parents work and the baby is cared for by other adults in another home or daycare center? Will parent and child be less attached; will the child suffer socially, emotionally, or mentally; and will the parent miss out on an experience that is as old as the species itself?

Parenthood is real work and there are many decisions to make. Yet while advice is plentiful, solid information to help parents make their own decisions is dear. Parents used to go to their own parents with questions about childrearing. But grandparents often live farther away now. And there are new questions parents face today—working mothers, daycare centers, and changing expectancies of what boys and girls should be like, to name a few. Today's family is not the same as yesterday's.

Surveys show that parents feel a greater need for help in raising their children today than a few years ago. As a result, there is a virtual explosion of books, magazine and newspaper articles, and television shows on how to raise kids, how to toilet train them, how to cope with single parenthood, how to teach your child to cook. But is that what new parents really want—ten easy rules for raising children or simple recipes for dealing with the problems that most children pose for their parents? Publishers think so, but parents might not.

Dr. Alison Clarke-Stewart of the University of Chicago asked people who were reading books about childcare what they hoped to gain from those materials. Most said they were *not* looking for advice on how to solve specific problems or help in making particular decisions. Rather, most wanted books to tell them about the normal process of infant and child development.

By and large, that is not exactly what most books dispense. Many are written by physicians, psychiatrists, and clinical psychologists who are widely experienced in dealing with medical and behavioral problems, especially those that prompt parents to seek professional help. They are specialists in the unusual child. Other books and articles are written by educators, journalists, and parents themselves who pass along tips they've acquired in their own personal experience with their particular children. That advice may or may not apply to the next parent and child. Other authors are advocates, admonishing parents to experience natural childbirth, to breast-feed their infants, not to take pap from the school system, and so forth. To be sure, these books and articles have a certain utility, and many of them are quite good. But Clarke-Stewart's survey reveals that most parents are not primarily interested in solving problems in other people's idiosyncratic experience, or in propaganda. They want to know how their infants and children grow and change, and how they can be an integral part of their baby's development.

This book attempts to provide such information about the first three years of life. It is not a "how-to" book, and for good reasons. There are no ten easy rules for trouble-free parenthood, at least not ten that are sufficiently specific to tell every parent what to do beyond love, respect, caring, and other commonsense platitudes. A prescription that will work for one parent-child pair may be totally wrong for another. What the parent needs is not more advice but the best information available about the normal course of infant development. Given a knowledge of what to expect and why, parents should be able to make better decisions on their own.

This book does not tell parents what to do or think as much as it tells them what to think about. It offers some information that will help readers make their own choices. I don't discuss caretaking chores—how to wash bottles, mix formula, treat colds, or what immunizations to give the child. Such information can be found in many sources. My emphasis instead is on the development of the person that is the infant—his or her personality, the emergence of love and attachment between parent and infant, the growth of intelligence, language, and social behavior.

During the last decade, research psychologists have intensively studied babies, and their research covers a host of questions that will interest anyone concerned with infants. What can a baby see or hear at birth? When infants look at a parent, what do they see—patterns of lights and colors or a face? Do babies dream? What considerations are important in deciding whether to breast- or bottle-feed? How often do babies eat, how long do they sleep, and when will they sleep through the night? What are the ways parents can communicate with their babies and how do their babies communicate with them? When do parents start to feel love for their infants, and what are the facts about the new hospital practice of parent-infant bonding? How early can an infant start to learn things? What effect does all this early stimulation have on a baby? Can one predict later IQ from infant tests? Do temperamental differences between babies forecast later personality? Why do infants show fear of strangers? What kind of toys and play do infants enjoy? How does a child acquire language? What makes two-year-olds negative with their parents and aggressive with their peers? In a real sense, this book is a report on the fascinating research that addresses these questions.

Rearing an infant can be an intellectually exciting and emotionally fulfilling responsibility. This book is dedicated to helping parents and infants realize these joys together.

I am grateful for the assistance and support of many. Father Flanagan's Boys Home and the Center for the Study of Youth Development, where I am employed, have encouraged this activity as part of their effort to disseminate research results that will contribute to the welfare of children, youth, and families everywhere. S. Holly Stocking provided valuable guidance in writing; Sandra Wendel proofed manuscript and galleys; and Bess Melvin and Pat Mordeson handled the clerical chores. I thank Dorothy Eichorn, Alexander Roche, Philip Salapatek, Alan Sroufe, and Ina Uzgiris for their helpful comments on portions of the manuscript, and William Kessen for his insightful overview. Finally, I appreciate the efforts of hundreds of scientists, graduate students, and assistants who have generated the research results reported in this volume, and I apologize if I have misrepresented those efforts in any way.

R.B.M.
Boys Town, Nebraska

Contents

Part One. How Infants Develop
   1. Understanding Development   3
   2. Milestones of Growth   12
Part Two. The World of the Newborn
   3. Biological Beginnings   29
   4. Preparation for Love and Attachment   49
Part Three. The First Year
   5. The Growth of Mentality   77
   6. Personality and the Growth of Attachment   102
Part Four. The Second Year
   7. First Words   131
   8. Social Development   146
Index   165
Credits   169

Part One
How Infants Develop

Chapter One
Understanding Development

IN THE BEGINNING, the cell is the size of a pinhead. But not for long. It doubles and redoubles, and redoubles again. This cluster of cells elongates and then curls in upon itself, and tissues that were once the same become different—muscles, bone, and skin emerge. In only eight weeks, the fetus has grown to one inch in length and has clearly identifiable facial features, a heart that beats sturdily, and even the rudiments of fingers and toes. After twelve weeks, and now weighing about an ounce, the fetus can kick its legs, close its fingers, squint, frown, and open its mouth. In another four weeks, the mother can begin to feel some of these fetal acrobatics. At this point, the fetus looks a lot like a very small baby. All of the body's systems are present down to hair on the head, sweat glands, and taste buds. Nevertheless, it will be another ten weeks before the fetus could survive outside the womb if it were born prematurely. And still fourteen weeks more before the human infant normally makes a wet and often noisy debut into the world. Although the drama of growth and development has been unfolding for nine months, birth marks the beginning of the first act that we are privileged to witness. The period of continuing life that we call infancy has just begun.

At least from Hippocrates to the 1860s, philosophers and scientists thought that development was simply the

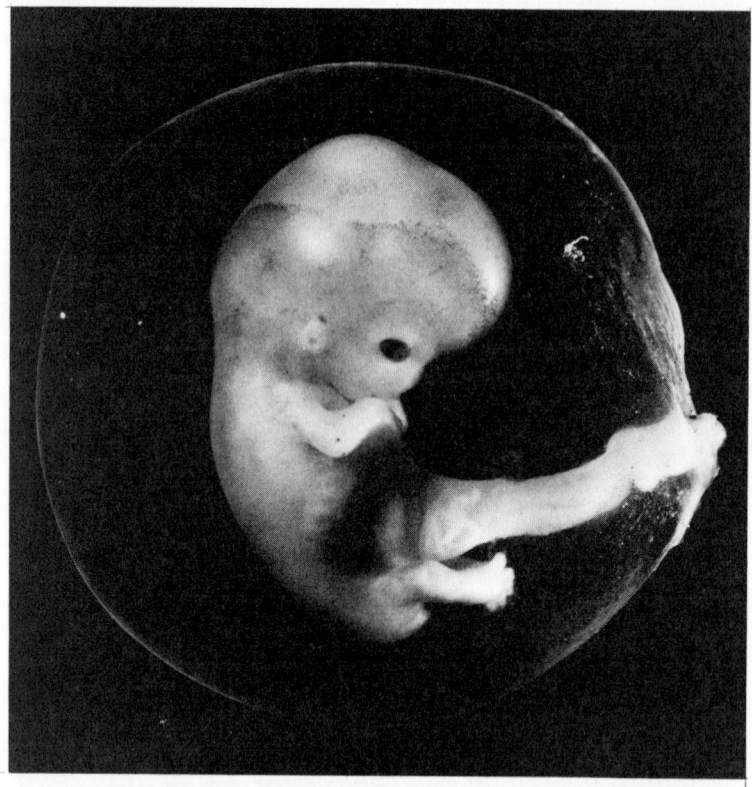

A six-week-old embryo is only about three quarters of an inch long and weighs about one fifth of an ounce.

process of growing bigger. They believed that the sex cells, especially the sperm, actually contained a completely formed, tiny adult called a *homunculus*. All that was required was time for the homunculus to grow bigger—nothing fundamentally changed from one stage to the next.

In 1677, the Dutch naturalist and microscopist, Antony van Leeuwenhoek, claimed he could tell the difference between the sperm destined to produce male animals and those destined to produce female animals, because the miniature creatures copulated on the slides of his microscope and the females gave birth to little animalcules. Other scientists claimed they could distinguish between the sperm of donkeys and horses because the tiny animals of one had longer ears than those of the other. According to these "preformationists," the human infant was simply an adult in miniature.

The belief in preformationism died when the Russian scientist D. F. Wolff published his studies on embryology. Wolff observed that embryos of different mammals looked very much alike in their early stages, but as they grew older, each species developed its own specific characteristics. Moreover, blood vessels and intestines were not initially present in the embryos of chicks —they developed out of tissue that originally bore no resemblance to these organs. Clearly, organisms were not totally preformed in every detail but changed their fundamental nature with development.

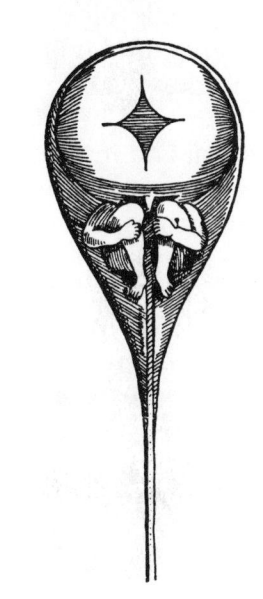

For centuries, scientists believed that each human spermatozoon contained a miniature individual, a homunculus.

Scientists found that the transformations Wolff and others had observed followed the same orderly sequence for each member of a species. Therefore, it was thought that development was *predetermined,* that such changes unfolded according to nature's plan regardless of the environment the organism was exposed to. For example, tadpoles swim at the appointed moment in development whether they are allowed to "practice" or not. In the 1930s and '40s, Dr. Arnold Gesell applied this view of development to the human child in a famous series of books for parents that is still widely read. According to Gesell, the child's physical ability, personality, and intelligence unfold in successive stages that are largely controlled by a maturational plan guided by the genes.

Today developmental scientists emphasize that both experience in the environment and genetic factors fixed by heredity play a necessary part in development. Neither part can be played without the other. The controversial and interesting questions concern how large a part each factor plays and how the two work together to shape each aspect of the child's development.

Heredity and Environment

The contribution of heredity and environment to the growth and development of an individual is one of history's oldest debates—and one of the least understood. Most people learn a little about heredity from high school biology classes that describe Gregor Mendel's experiments with plant breeding and tell us how the sex of a child is determined. Parents-to-be encounter it when they take blood tests for the presence of Rh factors or later when their baby is screened for phenylketonuria, a metabolic disorder found in one of every 10,000 births.

Many of us come away from these experiences with certain beliefs about how heredity operates. We tend to think that the characteristics of a person are either inherited or learned, not the product of both forces. Genes determine a baby's sex or adult height; but children acquire language through experience and learning. We also believe that once a trait is "in the genes," it is determined for life and cannot be changed. If you are destined to be five feet eleven, then that is what you will be and no amount of meat, potatoes, and green beans will change it.

Myths about Heredity

Fortunately, these are myths, especially when it comes to behavioral characteristics. Most aspects of social and mental behavior are not as directly influenced by heredity as are physical traits, but genes do influence behavior. For example, research indicates that hereditary factors contribute to sociability—whether a person is shy, withdrawn, and private or openly friendly, affable, and gregarious. In addition, genes appear to influence general mental performance as much as or more than any other behavior that scientists study. But these "influences" are not all or none, and in most cases the potential for learning and experience to make a difference is still quite great.

Parents will notice that each of their children is different from the others, almost from the very beginning. Their children will differ in activity, temperament, intelligence, interests, and personal style, and a portion of these differences is associated with their genetic heritage. But in contrast to many inherited physical traits, learning and experience play a greater role at nearly every stage of development.

The Effects of Early Experience

Ironically, many people hold similar beliefs about the effects of early experience—that it has an indelible and permanent influence on our lives. How often do we hear that the "early years are formative" or that "most of a child's intelligence is determined by the age of three or six years"? These extreme statements are also myths.

Modern thought concerning development has been influenced greatly by the writings of Sigmund Freud. Among other contributions, Freud emphasized how experiences early in the life of an individual could have enduring consequences on personality and social behavior. Freud's theorizing focused the attention of psychologists and educators on the importance of infancy and early experiences. The result has been a staunch belief by professionals and the public alike that somehow early experiences are more important than later experiences. Consequently, many parents believe that what they do with their child as an infant or toddler leaves an indelible imprint on them.

Predictions to adulthood are not perfect. Certainly early experiences can mold a child, but it is an exaggeration to assert that they necessarily mark a child for life and cannot be reversed. If personality and intelligence were cemented into an individual in the first few years of life, then one should be able to predict with considerable certainty the adult personalities and mental competencies of individuals on the basis of their characteristics at age two or four. It is true that adult intelligence becomes *more* predictable between the ages of two and six years, but the relationship is not so strong that change is impossible. For example, scientists at the Fels Research Institute in Yellow Springs, Ohio, administered intelligence tests to individuals throughout childhood, and found that the average child changed 28.5 IQ points between two and one-half and seventeen years of age. One in seven children shifted 40 points or more, and one child increased 74 IQ points, rising from the bottom 13 percent to the very top of the population. Moreover, these changes in IQ were not random fluctuations, but progressive, meaningful increases or decreases in mental performance. And these were normal, typical children from middle-class homes who received no special program or educational experience.

Recovery from deprivation. If early experience is so necessary to later development, how are we to explain the recovery of children who are tragically neglected or imprisoned for the first several years of life? In 1938, a girl who had been locked in a room until the age of six and a half was discovered in Ohio. Isabelle was the illegitimate child of a deaf mute, whose family confined mother and child together in a dark room. When she was discovered, Isabelle had rickets from the lack of sunshine and poor diet. Her legs were so bowed that when she stood erect the soles of her shoes did not rest on the floor but came flat together. Isabelle did not speak. Occasionally she communicated by croaks or gestures. When strangers approached, she became wild with fear and hostility. As one might expect, she did not know what to do with common toys. Instead of rolling or bouncing a ball, she stroked the face of her doctor with it. She was so unresponsive and inexperienced with sights and sounds that it took some time to determine if she could hear. Her behaviors were much like a six-month-old infant, and many thought she was feebleminded because she scored essentially zero on nonverbal as well as verbal tests of intelligence. Her scores on a social maturity scale placed her at approximately the level of a two-and-a-half-year-old. Most specialists concluded that she was totally beyond hope, could not be educated, and probably would never learn to speak after living so long in silence.

Drs. Marie Mason and Kingsley Davis tried anyway. In less than two years she was miraculously rehabilitated to almost normal tested intelligence and social responsiveness.

> It seemed hopeless at first. The approach had to be through pantomime and dramatization, suitable to an infant. It required one week of intensive effort before she even made her first attempt at vocalization. Gradually she began to respond, however, and, after the first hurdles had at last been overcome, a curious thing happened. She went through the usual stages of learning characteristic of the years from one to six not only in proper succession but far more rapidly than normal. In a little over two months after her first vocalization she was putting sentences together. Nine months after that she could identify words and sen-

tences on the printed page, could write well, could add to ten, and could retell a story after hearing it. Seven months beyond this point she had a vocabulary of 1,500–2,000 words and was asking complicated questions. Starting from an educational level of between one and three years (depending on what aspect one considers), she had reached a normal level by the time she was eight and a half years old. In short she covered in two years the stages of learning that ordinarily require six. Or, to put it another way, her I.Q. trebled in a year and a half . . .

When the writer saw Isabelle a year and a half after her discovery, she gave him the impression of being a very bright, cheerful, energetic little girl. She spoke well, walked and ran without trouble, and sang with gusto and accuracy. Today she is over fourteen years old and has passed the sixth grade in a public school. Her teachers say that she participates in all school activities as normally as other children. (From K. Davis, "Final Note on a Case of Extreme Isolation," *American Journal of Sociology*, 1947, *45*, 554–565. Davis quotes Mason's original article, "Learning To Speak after Six and a Half Years of Silence," *Journal of Speech Disorders*, 1942, *7*, 295–304.)

Fortunately such cases are rare, but Isabelle is not the only instance. Drs. Ann M. and A. D. B. Clarke at the University of Hull in England have edited a volume, *Early Experience: Myth and Evidence*, documenting several other cases in which children have been inhumanly deprived; many have made substantial improvement with therapy. Nevertheless, nature is not totally forgiving. Total deprivation for more than eight or ten years might lead to permanent, irrevocable disability. Among normally reared children, however, mental and social characteristics are not obviously fixed at three, four, or even six years of age.

Implications for parents. Intelligence is one of the more stable characteristics known to psychologists, and heredity seems to play a greater role in its development than most other behaviors. Yet substantial and sometimes amazing changes in mental test performance have been observed for certain individuals. The potential for change appears even greater for social behavior and personality. While research reveals a modest consistency in some characteristics, such as sociability, more change than consistency takes place in social behavior and personality between infancy and childhood or adulthood.

Therefore parents should not get too excited when their child walks or talks early, because that fact alone does not predict later mental ability. Similarly, if a child is slow to crawl or say a first word, one should not be too alarmed. It is more likely than not that things will turn out reasonably well.

This is not to say that an experience will be equally effective no matter how old the child is at the time. It is often easier to teach certain behaviors and establish certain attitudes early in a child's life than it is to do so later. The situation is somewhat akin to learning to play tennis: it is easier for a child than an adult to acquire the proper way to serve and hit a forehand and backhand, especially if the adult must unlearn improper movements or bad habits first. Nevertheless, it is possible to be a late bloomer in tennis and many other skills, if the desire is strong enough.

In the remaining pages of this book, we will come to understand how the infant's inherited dispositions, abilities, and limitations are carefully orchestrated with environmental experiences to promote development. Development is not simply a process in which the infant grows bigger and more capable, but one in which the very nature of the person undergoes dramatic changes. When a new stage of development is reached, new abilities are savored and exercised. Many experiences are vital for development, but they must be carefully matched with the child's skills and interests at a given point in development. Fortunately, nature conspires to bring experience and infant together at the right time, and there is a great tolerance for error.

Chapter Two
Milestones of Growth

EVERYONE IS CURIOUS about physical growth. After all, growing is one of the most impressive things a young infant does. But people often misunderstand the significance of sheer growth. Bigger is not necessarily better—either at birth or at the first birthday. Early sitting, standing, and walking don't predict later physical coordination very well, and they don't predict later mental ability at all.

Parents do a lot of unnecessary worrying about physical growth, and probably some unwarranted bragging as well. It turns out that there is a very wide range of normal development, and once parents know what to expect, they will rarely have cause for concern.

Growth in Physical Size

Although infants may lose weight during the first few days or weeks, the average newborn will gain almost 130 percent in weight during the first six months of life (a little more for males and a little less for females). The growth rate slows down thereafter. Weight gain amounts to only 30–33 percent between six and twelve months of life, and the average toddler will gain another 45½ percent between one and three years of life.

With respect to height (actually length, because infants are measured lying on their backs), infants grow approximately 33 percent during the first six months, 12–13 percent during the next six months, and 27 percent between the ages of one and three years.

This is an astonishing rate of growth, and we can be grateful that it slows down as quickly as it does. If growth continued at the rate typical of the first six months of life, the average ten-year-old would check in at approximately 100 feet tall and weigh roughly 240,000 *tons*. That is as tall as some fifteen-story office buildings and twenty times heavier!

Growth Charts

The graphs shown here are the physical growth standards from birth to thirty-six months as published by the National Center for Health Statistics of the United States Department of Health, Education, and Welfare. Each graph contains three curves. The heavy line indicates the median length or weight for children of a given age. Half the children will fall above and half below these values. The dashed line above the median represents the top 5 percent, while the dashed line below the median indicates the lowest 5 percent of children.

These data come from one of the largest, most broadly based longitudinal studies of infants and children in the world conducted at the Fels Research Institute in Yellow Springs, Ohio. The charts are considered the American standards for growth, and they are presumed to reflect typical growth patterns for many portions of Western Europe as well. However, just as boys and girls differ in length and weight, so do certain racial groups within and between countries.

Using the charts. Parents are often curious about how tall or heavy their infant is, and often they are only able to compare their child with one or two other infants in their family or neighborhood. These charts provide a more accurate and representative standard for this purpose, although parents should not run to their

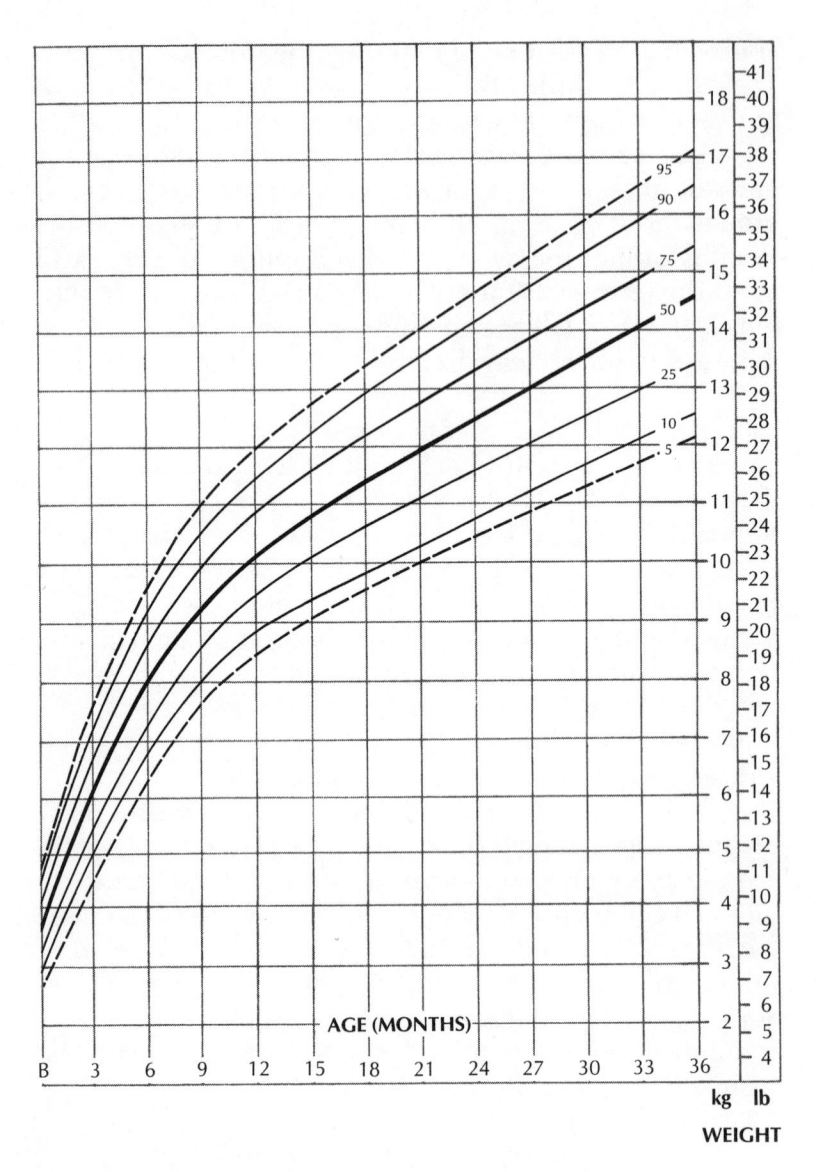

Weight chart for boys from birth to 36 months.

pediatrician if their child is below the median. However, if a child is in the highest or lowest 5 percent (outside the dashed lines), parents may ask the pediatrician to measure the child at the next checkup. It is important to remember that 5 percent of quite healthy infants will be above the top line and 5 percent below the bottom line—children are not necessarily abnormal if they exceed these values.

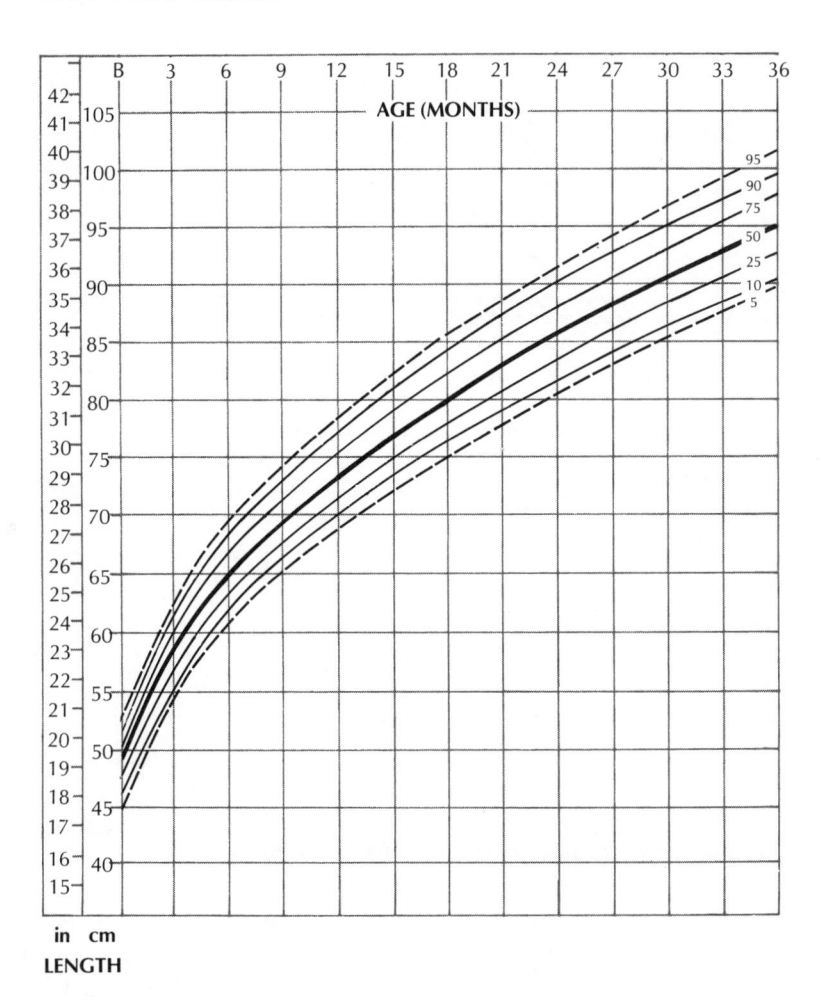

Length chart for boys from birth to 36 months.

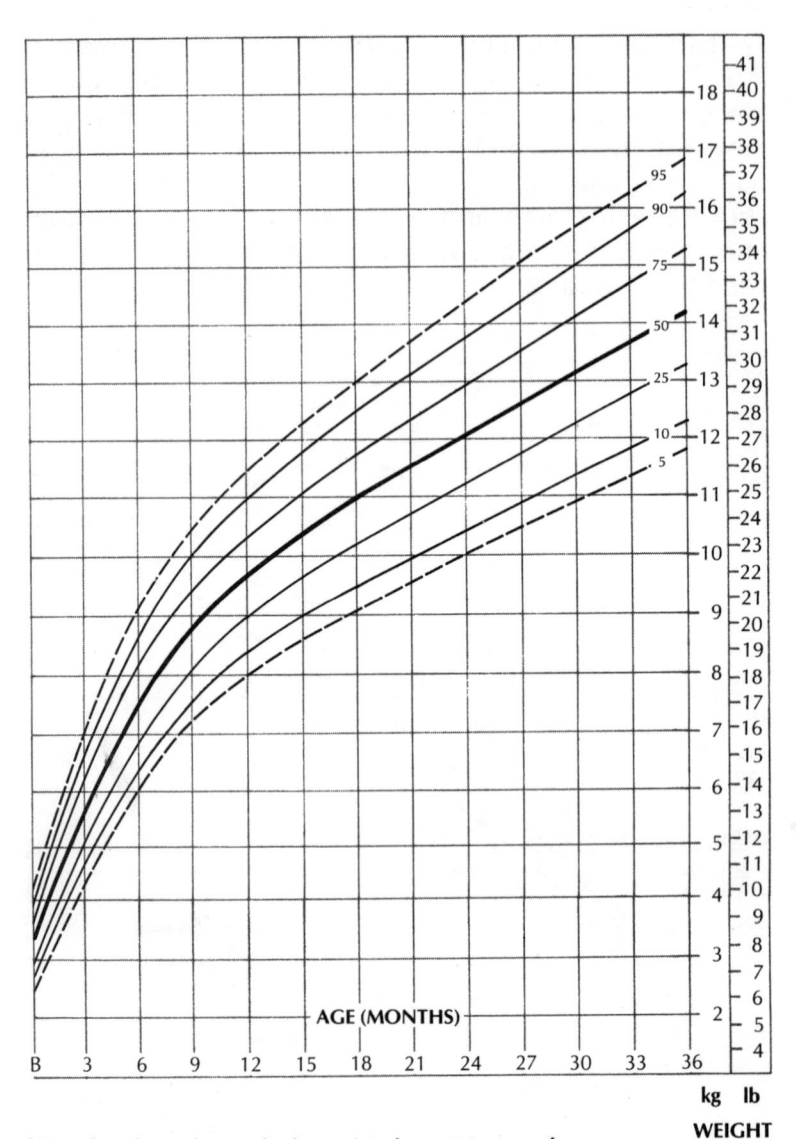

Weight chart for girls from birth to 36 months.

From a health standpoint, it is probably more important to chart a child's physical growth over age than to concern oneself with how long or heavy the infant is at any single age. Infants do not necessarily stay tall or small over the course of infancy, especially during the first year of life. Also, a serious illness can momentarily slow growth, but a resurgence may follow that actually helps the child "catch up" to where he or she would have been had the illness not occurred.

Predicting adult size. Parents inevitably wonder how big their infant will be as an adult. Some parents even assume that a high birth weight forecasts a large

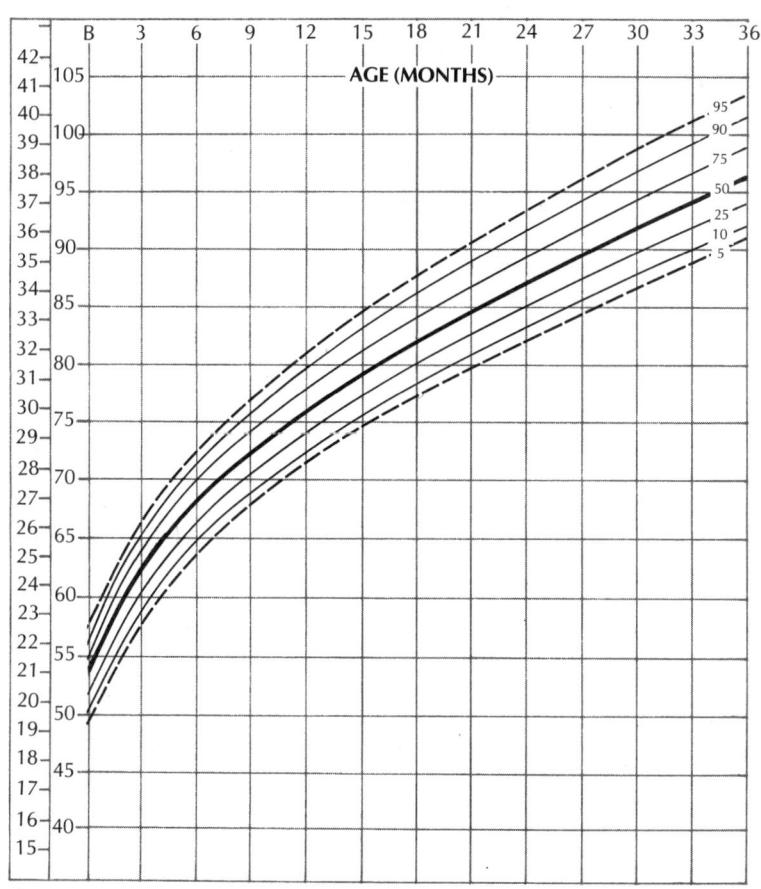

Length chart for girls from birth to 36 months.

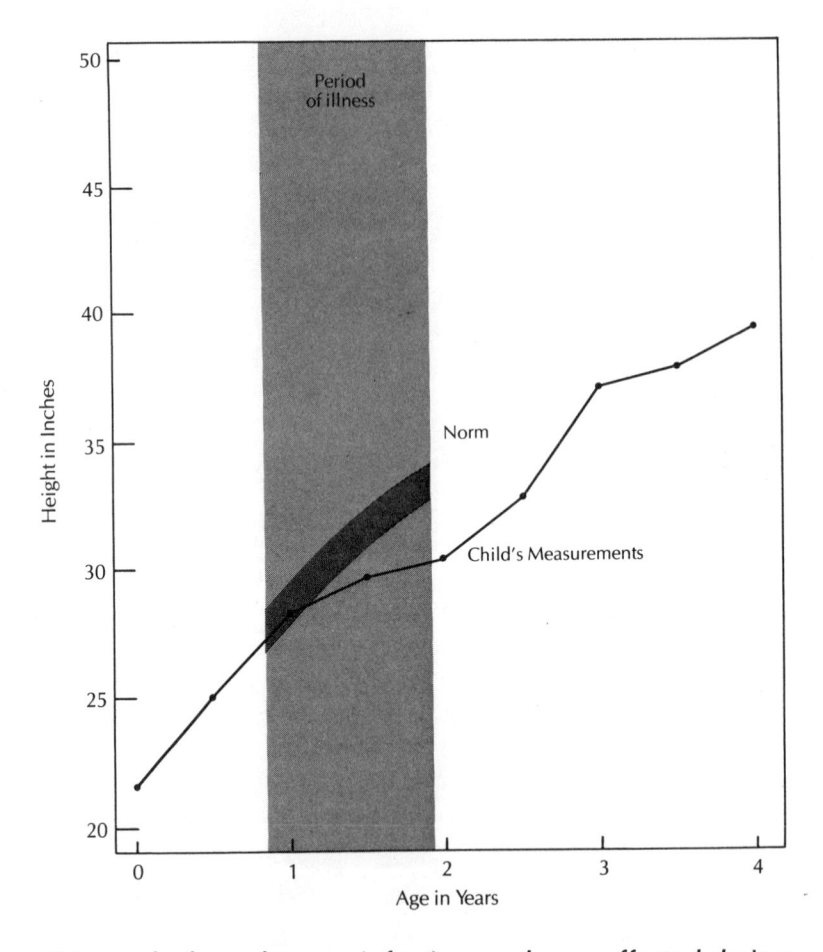

This graph shows how an infant's growth was affected during a year-long illness. The rate of growth slowed down during the illness, but accelerated to compensate for lost time as soon as normal eating patterns were restored.

child. The truth of the matter is that, if an infant is considered to be of normal size at birth, birth weight reveals very little about the child's potential height and weight. At birth a child's weight is partly determined by the size of the mother, which is nature's way of ensuring that mother and infant have an easier time during delivery. For example, if the genes of a fetus dictate a large size but the mother is relatively small, the fetus will grow more slowly during the last few weeks before birth to accommodate the smaller mother. Alternatively, such a slowing of fetal growth may not occur for that infant if plenty of room is available in the uterus. In the case of twins, the decline in growth rate near the end of pregnancy may be quite marked because of the relatively cramped quarters prior to birth. After delivery, infants who have slowed down because of a small mother may show a slight growth spurt, as if to make up for lost time.

This accommodation to maternal size occurs in other animals as well. For example, if large Shire horses are crossed with small Shetlands, the foals born to Shire mothers will be larger than those born to Shetland mothers. However, after a few months, offspring from both mothers will be approximately the same size.

While it is not possible to predict adult size from birth weight, a little more can be said by the time the child is one year old. Children substantially above the median at this time are likely to be above the median as adults, and, conversely, children substantially below the median at one year are likely to be below the median as adults. But there are exceptions, many of them. Even if the child is not an exception, being above or below the median is not saying much. Half the readers of this book are themselves below the median—which is what the median means.

What Influences Growth?

Most of us feel that height is genetically determined and that nothing can be done about it. It is true that the vast majority of the differences between the heights of adults are associated with differences in their genetic composition. On the other hand, all so-called genetic characteristics are dependent to some extent on a certain environment for their development. Therefore the issue is not whether a trait like physical growth can be changed, but rather how easily it can be changed.

Diet. Diet makes some difference. The average height in the United States, Europe, and Japan has been increasing over recent decades. Specialists in physical growth speculate that these increments are associated with higher nutritional, medical, and public health standards in these societies, but this is difficult to prove. The increasing trend for Americans and some other societies is leveling off, and some scientists feel that the Americans' genetic stock has achieved its maximum growth potential under contemporary nutritional and medical circumstances. In contrast, the average height in Sweden, Japan, and Holland continues to increase, while it is decreasing in parts of India.

Nutrition may make its most important contribution prenatally. Diet during pregnancy has always been regarded as important, and it still is. Despite the wide availability of adequate food supplies in industrial societies, not every pregnant woman eats properly. If there is a shortage of certain nutritional elements in the mother's system, nature serves the fetus first and the mother gets the leftovers. However, first call on a limited supply may still constitute inadequate nutrition and lead to birth complications, dangerously small birth size, and possibly smaller adult size.

A child's height can potentially be altered by giving certain hormones that control the growth process. Such therapy is most effective around the time of puberty, and it is easier to accelerate than to retard growth. However, these drugs may change the person's height by only an inch or so, hormone extracts are expensive, and undesirable side effects may occur. Consequently, these treatment programs are pursued only in the case of severe physical or psychological circumstances.

Prematurity. Although birth weight does not predict adult size for most babies, infants who are extremely small at birth may remain somewhat small throughout life.

Until recently, any child who was born lighter than 2500 grams (5.5 pounds) was labeled "premature." But medical science has found that such babies were not all actually born before their time. Also, medical advances have enabled many small babies to survive who might not have had they been born some years ago. Therefore, today an infant weighing less than 2000 grams (4.4 pounds) is called "an infant of low birth weight."

Infants may be unusually small for two reasons. Some are of low birth weight because they are young. That is, they have less than the average forty-week gestational tenure in the womb and are small only because they have had less time to grow. These are "true prematures." Often these infants are quite healthy; they are simply small, and they eventually catch up to infants who are not of low birth weight. Of course, in the case of infants born extraordinarily early (before twenty-seven to twenty-eight weeks), survival can be touch and go. But, with these exceptions, true premature infants typically do quite well.

Some infants are of low birth weight for reasons other than short gestation and are called "small for gestational age" or "small for dates" to distinguish them from true prematures. The circumstance that has caused the small size of these infants is more likely to affect their future growth potential. Actually, most such babies grow up quite normally. As a group, they do tend to be slightly shorter than other children, but the difference is only a few centimeters (about an inch) on the average.

Bigger and sooner are not necessarily better. Parents often want their infant to grow up quickly. In part, these desires are understandable. All parents want their infants to be healthy and to grow normally, and the completion of developmental milestones (such as weaning and sleeping through the night) often spells the end of exhausting routines for parents. But for many parents "health" means "large," even plump, and normal developmental progress becomes "sooner is better." These are not necessarily appropriate interpretations.

Obesity is a major national health problem in many industrial countries, and one interesting but hotly contested theory states that early feeding practices are a possible contributor to later overweight. We know that fat adults have approximately twice as many fat cells as thin adults. Moreover, experiments with animals seem to indicate that early diet determines the number of fat cells the organism will have for the remainder of its life. If this is also true of humans, then it is possible that overeating by mothers during the last trimester of pregnancy and overfeeding of infants during the first four months of life, periods in which the number of fat cells rises most rapidly, might dispose the child toward obesity later in life. Further, when people gain or lose weight, it is the amount of fat in each fat cell, not the number of cells, that appears to change. Therefore some scientists believe that individuals who have more fat cells that inflate easily with an improper diet are disposed toward being overweight.

Whether or not this theory is true, it is a mistake to over- or underfeed infants during these important growth periods, especially to restrict severely the intake of fats that are required for the growth of the nervous system. Some people feel that babies should eat a lot to be healthy, but given what we are learning about obesity, a better rule is probably "moderation in all things." There is usually no need to "encourage" an infant to eat—no one has heard of a normal infant who deliberately refuses to eat for very long. A similar problem occurs later in infancy when some parents are anxious to get their children onto solid food as soon as possible. One reason for this eagerness is that feeding solids at night may help the child sleep through until morning. But some recent evidence indicates that feeding solids, particularly meats, too early in the child's development may increase the likelihood of certain allergies.

Finally, although certain segments of the American population are deficient in vitamins A and C, and in iron and riboflavin among other nutrients, excesses of these substances are common among other groups. Again, more is not necessarily better. In one study of American infants 22–23 months of age, from 36 percent to 84 percent of the children were taking vitamin supplements (depending on their social class) and these percentages declined only slightly between 24–35 months. Children in the middle and upper social classes were literally taking twice as many vitamins as the recommended daily allowances of the American National Academy of Science. The body tends to excrete some excess vitamins, but it does not necessarily pass all, and some research suggests that too much of certain vitamins may be detrimental to infants. Again, moderation seems in order. If the infant is consistently getting a balanced diet, vitamin supplements are unnecessary and possibly harmful.

Motor Development

An infant's first step is often the cause of great celebration. Actually, there are many developmental markers on the road to running and jumping, and they fall into a rather predictable sequence.

Developmental Milestones

Table 1 shows the average age at which a few of these skills are accomplished, plus the age range within which 90 percent of American children first display the behavior. Once again, parents are advised to curb their excitement or their concern if their child falls near one end or the other of this range. The age at which walking or talking first occurs reveals very little about that child's later physical or mental accomplishments. At this age, the physical and mental characteristics of the child's parents are more predictive of success in these areas

Table 1. Physical Milestones in Infancy

Behavior	Age Range in Months	Average Age in Months
Raises self by arms while lying face down	.7–5	2.1
Sits with support	1–5	2.3
Sits alone momentarily	4–8	5.3
Sits alone for 30 seconds or more	5–8	6.0
Rolls from back to stomach	4–10	6.4
Sits alone quite steadily for long periods	5–9	6.6
Stands up holding onto furniture	6–12	8.6
Walks while adult holds hands	7–12	9.6
Sits down after standing	7–14	9.6
Stands alone	9–16	11.0
Walks alone	9–17	11.7
Walks sideways	10–20	14.1
Walks backward	11–20	14.6
Walks up stairs with help	12–23	16.1
Stands on left foot alone	15–30+	22.7
Jumps off floor with both feet	17–30+	23.4
Stands on right foot alone	16–30+	23.5
Jumps from the last stair step to floor	19–30+	24.8
Walks up stairs alone with both feet on each step	18–30+	25.1
Walks a few steps on tiptoes	16–30+	25.7
Walks down stairs alone with both feet on each step	19–30+	25.8
Jumps from the second stair step to the floor	21–30+	28.1
Walks up stairs alternating forward foot	23–30+	30+

From the Bayley Scales of Infant Development, *Motor Scale Record* (The Psychological Corporation, 1969).

than almost any characteristic of the child. Parents rarely go around saying that their nine-month-old infant is going to be a genius because they themselves are brilliant, but if they did they would actually be on firmer scientific ground than if they made such predictions based on early walking or talking.

The appropriateness of the age ranges in Table 1 depends upon a variety of circumstances. For example, boys may achieve some of these milestones at different ages than girls; blacks tend to be slightly more precocious than whites in some skills; fat and thin children may reach certain levels at different ages. The age norms may also depend on the child's nationality. Research reported by Dr. Colin B. Hindley at the University of London turned up the odd fact that children in Brussels and Stockholm walked about one month earlier, and were more advanced in other aspects of motor development, than children in Paris, London, and Zurich.

EXPERIENCE AND TRAINING

For the most part, the timing and sequence of the steps outlined in Table 1 unfolds according to nature's plan because most children are reared in adequate environments. Nevertheless, while almost all children follow the same sequence, some children reach various levels ahead of others. The wide age ranges for normal children testify to substantial individual differences from one child to the next, even within the same family. A few classic studies exist in which the early opportunities for physical exercise of one or both members of a pair of twins were restricted to determine whether this would affect the age at which walking and other physical milestones occurred. Typically, the restricted twin did not crawl or walk precisely at the same age as the exercised twin, but after a few days of encouragement and practice the restricted twin was typically back on schedule.

But if children are reared under very poor conditions, substantial delays in crawling and walking can occur. Dr. Wayne Dennis of the City University of New York found an orphanage in the Middle East where infants had only one caregiver for every eight children. No time was spent playing with the infants or giving them encouragement, and almost no social interaction occurred. These children first sat alone at approximately two years of age (almost 18 months later than the average in Table 1), and only 15 percent could walk alone by four years of age (the average age is 11.7 months under normal family circumstances). However, when toys were provided and the children were encouraged to play with them, they started to develop normally. The potential for achieving physical accomplishments is largely governed by the child's own maturational clock, but whether a given infant performs them or not at a specific age requires a little exercise and encouragement.

If it is possible to hasten the age of walking by a few weeks, is it desirable to do so? At present, no particular evidence indicates that infants are harmed by moderate, appropriate exercise, but neither is there evidence to suggest that early programs of intensive encouragement are particularly beneficial later. No one has demonstrated that early walking leads to more advanced accomplishment of any valued skill later in childhood or adulthood. Many experienced parents will advise to the contrary—early walking only means that children get into everything in the home sooner. Perhaps the best guide is for parents and infants to have a good time together, exercising or not exercising, and for parents not to worry about their child's developmental progress. Given any of a wide range of "normal" environments, physical development will usually take care of itself.

Part Two
The World of the Newborn

Chapter Three
Biological Beginnings

IN RELATION TO OTHER MAMMALS, the human infant is one of the more helpless creatures at birth. But we should not assume that the infant is totally unprepared for life outside the womb. In this chapter we will explore the newborn's ability to survive—to regulate temperature, to eat, to sleep, and to respond to certain stimuli. As we will see, in all these matters the infant is remarkably well organized and prepared to deal with the world.

Maintaining the Right Temperature

Human beings are warm-blooded. Although it is true that warm-blooded animals do have warmer blood than cold-blooded species, the important point is that warm-blooded organisms attempt to regulate their temperature. In the human infant, temperature regulation is a crucial task because enzymes, which are protein substances that regulate food processing and metabolism, operate effectively only at certain temperatures. If the body is too cold, metabolic functions might slow down and literally "starve" the infant; if the temperature is too high, a physiological thermostat shuts off all enzyme activity. In either extreme, the infant's body is denied the nutrition needed for survival.

When adults are too hot, their metabolic rate slows down; their blood vessels dilate, allowing more blood to the surface of the body where heat can be dissipated into the air; they sweat, losing heat through evaporation; and they pant, expelling heat in the air that is exhaled. In contrast, if adults are too cold, their metabolic rate increases, producing more body heat; their blood vessels constrict, sending blood away from the surface toward the center of the body; and they shiver and move around to keep warm.

The task of regulating temperature is more difficult for newborn infants. Many of the adult's mechanisms depend on the surface area of the skin and metabolism—the burning of calories obtained in food. But the infant has more surface area per unit of weight than the adult does. At approximately two weeks of age, the average newborn weighs only 4.8 percent of what the average adult weighs, but the infant's skin area amounts to 15 percent of the adult's body surface. So the infant's potential for heat loss is much greater, and relatively more calories are required to keep the body warm. On the other side of the issue, infants who are too warm can cool down more rapidly than adults through sweating and hyperventilation, although they risk dehydration and the resulting production of excess body acids.

In addition to requiring relatively more calories simply to keep warm, the infant is growing at an incredible rate, as we have seen. But the infant's ability to take in calories is restricted because of the lack of teeth and the inability of the digestive system to deal with solid foods. Consequently, the newborn must ingest all calories in the form of milk. If adults were so restricted, we would have to force down 10–20 liters (or quarts) of milk per day on the basis of equal body weight. Moreover, this much liquid produces an enormous excess of water that must be filtered by the kidneys, which are among the least developed organs at birth. Small wonder that feeding and diapering are such major activities for the parents of a newborn.

Despite the fact that the baby's potential for heat loss is four times that of an adult, newborns are able to deal with the situation. For example, shortly after birth, premature as well as full-term infants respond to cold by constricting surface blood vessels, increasing the production of heat, and shivering. If too hot, blood will be shunted to the surface of their bodies; they will sweat and even pant. By two or three hours of life, the infant's response to cold is as good as that of an adult, at least relative to its body weight.

The newborn infant must be able to handle cold even at the moment of birth. Having spent all of its days in a liquid environment of approximately 37 degrees C (98.6 degrees F), the newborn is suddenly thrust out into a delivery room temperature that is inevitably colder—ranging from 15 to 28 degrees (59 to 82.4 degrees). Moreover, the infant is wet, and the evaporation of these fluids and of water from one or two baths increases the potential heat loss. But a normal infant survives this shock, despite the fact that heat must be generated at twice the adult rate to keep warm.

Parents need only a little common sense to help their infant maintain a proper temperature. Normal infants between 2270 and 3630 grams (5–8 pounds) will do quite nicely in a room approximately 21 degrees C (70 degrees F) with two light wool blankets and cotton sleeping clothes. When a child gets to weigh approximately 3630 grams (8 pounds), a little more insulating fat is available and temperatures can go as low as 15.6 C (60 degrees F) if the child has a sweater and two or three light blankets. It is just as important for infants to avoid extreme heat as it is for them to avoid cold, since enzyme functioning shuts down when the temperature is too high. Some pediatricians believe that infants may lose some of their ability to regulate temperature if they are always kept extremely warm.

Feeding

Another major task of the newborn is to obtain enough food to keep warm and to grow. The infant must take in enormous quantities of milk. Because newborns sleep a great deal and because their stomachs hold only a small amount relative to their requirements, they naturally spend most of their waking hours eating.

Sucking

Most people assume that sucking is an instinct. It is—but one that can be modified through learning. It is also a fantastically intricate behavior despite its apparent simplicity.

There are two basic components to sucking. The first is *negative pressure,* the vacuum created inside the mouth. When adults suck on a straw, they create an oral vacuum by drawing in air to the lungs. In contrast, infants usually produce negative pressure by closing off the oral cavity in the back of the mouth, sealing the lips and gums up front, and then dropping the lower jaw. Actually infants apparently know best, because their way makes it easier to synchronize sucking, swallowing, and breathing while avoiding getting liquid down the wrong pipe.

The second component of sucking is called *expressing*. The infant presses the nipple against the roof of the mouth and laps the tongue from the front to the rear of the mouth, thus pushing out the fluid. This tongue-rolling action may begin with a little bite, a fact that some breast-feeding mothers painfully discover.

Initially, the infant may be a little clumsy at integrating negative pressure, expressing, swallowing, and breathing together in a smooth sequence without having to drop the nipple to come up for air. But it is worked out soon. First, infants swallow faster than adults, in about .5 seconds as opposed to 1.5 seconds. Second, infants discover that a suck can be made at the same time air is taken in, a feat made possible by the way they produce negative pressure. Third, infants swallow between inhaling and exhaling. The typical infant integrates these actions into a smooth sequence in a week or two.

Infants tend to put their own personal stamp on their sucking behavior in the form of rhythm. Usually, infants suck in bursts separated by pauses. On the average, an infant will suck 5 to 24 times in a stretch, at a rate of approximately 1 to 2.5 sucks per second before resting a moment. Just how many sucks and how fast they occur within a burst will depend on the infant's level of hunger, age, health, time since last feeding, and degree of wakefulness. Parents will observe that infants pause less at the beginning of a feed than near the end, and that each infant has an individual style and pattern.

The Psychological Importance of Feeding

Freud thought that adult personalities could be traced to infant feeding patterns. Among other things he believed that gratifying oral experiences would result in "oral optimism," which includes an extroverted social character, generosity, and receptivity to new ideas. He felt that breast feeding was superior to bottle feeding in this regard. In contrast, if early oral gratification were frustrated in some way, "oral pessimism" would result, producing an aggressive, impatient, selfish, and insecure adult. More recently, Eric Eriksen, the well-known theorist on child development and personality, has suggested that oral experiences are vital in the development of a basic trust in people.

The problem with such theories is that psychological science has been unable to verify them. Dr. Bettye Caldwell of the University of Arkansas, an expert on infant care, points out that while some studies have shown better social adjustment in breast-fed babies, other research fails to demonstrate this. She concludes that the feeding experience does not obviously determine a pattern of psychological adjustment, personality, or social behavior.

While individual cases do not necessarily prove a point, the story of Monica is instructive. For medical reasons, Monica was fed from birth through a fistula, an artificial opening in her side. Obviously, she had little or no oral experience, at least none associated with feeding. Psychoanalysts predicted dire consequences for Monica. Presumably, as an adult she would be aggressive, insecure, impatient, and perhaps lack trust in other people.

Today Monica is a mother herself. She has none of the characteristics that were predicted. In fact, no one would suspect that she had such a profound experience as an infant. The only atypical behavior she has exhibited is that she bottle-fed her own baby as the infant lay flat on her lap rather than the more common position of resting against the chest in the crook of the adult's arms. Since this is the way Monica herself was fed, perhaps even this behavior is understandable. Early oral experiences, even highly serious departures from the average, do not seem to exert much of an influence on a child's personality development.

Breast or Bottle

In many respects breast feeding represents one of nature's beautiful matches between infant and environment. But some women are unable or prefer not to breast-feed for physical, medical, or psychological reasons. Still others must be away from their babies for long periods of time. Most women have some choice in the matter. There is much commotion about the virtues of breast feeding. What are the facts?

Breast milk is better than prepared formulas. This argument has some validity. First, breast-milk has certain immunizing characteristics that prepared formulas lack. Colostrum, the yellowish liquid secreted by the breast for the first few days of nursing, contains substances that provide some immunization against infections. In certain less developed countries, this is decidedly beneficial; in highly industrialized nations, where disease is under greater control, the advantage is less pronounced (although no one argues that formulas are better in this regard).

Second, the protein composition of breast milk is somewhat better than that of formulas. Milk contains two kinds of protein—lactalbumin, which is more easily digested and better for growth than the other type, casein. Human milk has more of the beneficial lactalbumin than formulas. Third, breast milk has fewer calories than formulas. Although newborns have a great need for calories, it is possible for the infant to get too many. Some pediatricians claim they have never seen a fat breast-fed infant. Of course, not every bottle-fed baby is overweight.

Breast milk is purer. Mother's milk is manufactured under hygienically perfect conditions, but formulas are certainly safe and sanitary by any standards. The real issue of purity pertains more to the delivery system than to the food itself. And just as one must keep bottles and nipples clean, mothers who nurse must also practice good body hygiene.

It is sometimes argued that the cow's milk in formulas contains a variety of contaminants—pesticides used to control insects, chemical fertilizers, or pollutants in the water cattle drink. Such claims are often exaggerated. For example, chemical analyses reveal more DDT in human milk than in cow's milk, but the absolute amounts in either are quite safe.

More important is the argument that mother's milk may not always be quite so pure as people think. One professional who is particularly concerned about toxic substances in breast milk is Dr. Jay M. Arena, professor of pediatrics at Duke University School of Medicine and director of the Poison Control Center there. Arena points out that almost anything the mother ingests can be detected in breast milk, although her body filters out most substances so that only small amounts remain in the milk. However, one needs to remember that the infant is approximately one twelfth of the body weight of the mother, so that even if only one twelfth of a toxic substance is passed through in breast milk, the dosage to the infant will be equivalent to that taken by the mother.

Although most women know they must not take potent medication while lactating, they are less aware that common substances, such as the nicotine in cigarette smoke, alcohol, caffeine in coffee and tea, and hormones in oral contraceptives, can be potentially harmful to the infant. For example, a woman who smokes ten to twenty cigarettes per day passes approximately .4 to .5 mg of nicotine in each liter of breast milk, which is equivalent to 6 to 7.5 mg of nicotine for the adult. While this is only a tenth of the lethal dose, even 4 mg of nicotine can produce pronounced symptoms in adults. And some lactating mothers have noticed that their infants are more irritable when they drink a lot of coffee. Although the evidence is not totally conclusive, Arena suggests that women who nurse should restrict their intake of cigarettes, coffee, alcohol, and oral contraceptives, and they should consult a physician before taking other medication.

Breast feeding has more psychological benefits. This is perhaps the most hotly contested claim, and a good answer is that it depends on the mother. For some, the intimacy of breast feeding is an incomparable human experience. Others find breast feeding embarrassing and a source of tension and self-doubt about their adequacy as a mother. The best course is for the mother to follow her own personal feelings: what is comfortable for the mother probably will be comfortable for the infant.

There are some claimed disadvantages to breast feeding:

Breasts will lose their shape. There is no conclusive evidence that this is true. When a woman's figure declines after three or four breast-fed children, the changes may stem from her advancing age rather than from breast feeding. Actually a small-breasted woman may gain a little fullness of bosom after lactating.

Breast feeding is more restrictive. Breast feeding may be *less* restrictive in getting about town *with* one's infant. However, if a mother must be away from her infant, at work for example, total reliance on breast feeding is very difficult. Breast feeding can be restrictive for nonworking mothers as well. First, a total regimen of breast feeding means that the mother is constantly on call and the father misses the opportunity to feed the infant. Second, American women tend to be more shy about breast feeding in the company of others than their European counterparts, and, therefore they are often inconvenienced by having to seek privacy while nursing.

What choice to make. The choice is mostly up to the mother. There may be some health benefit in breast feeding, and some women derive great satisfaction from the experience. However, women who would feel uncomfortable or who cannot breast-feed should remain secure in the fact that there are millions of healthy, well-adjusted mothers and infants who have used bottles.

Schedule or Self-Demand

At one time, mothers were advised to feed their babies every four hours no matter when the baby appeared hungry. More recent advice suggests that infants be fed on demand rather than on schedule.

Every four hours? A first question is how appropriate is the suggested four-hour schedule? For example, if infants are allowed to eat whenever they wish, how often do normal infants want to be fed? According to one study, about 60 percent of two-week-old infants prefer a three-hour schedule, while 60 percent of ten-

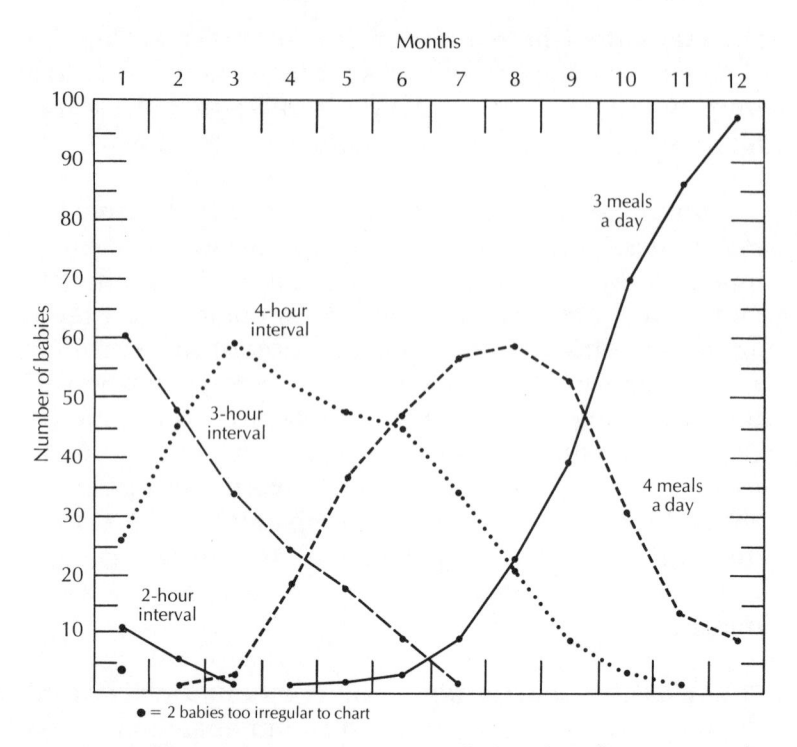

[Chart: Number of babies vs. Months, showing curves for 2-hour interval, 3-hour interval, 4-hour interval, 4 meals a day, and 3 meals a day. ● = 2 babies too irregular to chart]

Not all infants need or want to be fed at four-hour intervals. One hundred infants, fed on demand, chose this wide range of eating patterns.

week-old infants want to be fed every four hours. By seven or eight months of age, 60 percent were eating four meals a day, and most ten-month-old infants were having three meals a day. It is clear that the required number of feedings changed dramatically with age, and that approximately 40 percent of the infants did not follow the four-hour regimen. Therefore some attention must be paid to differences between infants.

But if an infant is allowed free demand of food, won't it become "spoiled"? Most contemporary opinion is that self-demand feeding per se does not produce spoiled children. In fact, the opposite may be true, especially during the first six months of life. Research by

Drs. Mary Ainsworth and Sylvia Bell, at Johns Hopkins University and the University of Virginia, suggests that infants whose needs are not promptly met are actually less secure, less attached to their parents, and perhaps more fretful than infants whose feeding and social needs are attended to right away. One explanation for these findings goes like this: Infants whose cries are not heeded tend to cry more vigorously and louder until their needs are satisfied. A child may come to learn that only loud cries bring results while modest signals for assistance are ignored. As a result, lusty crying is rewarded and increases in frequency.

Eventually, but probably not before seven or eight months of age, an infant can learn to control a parent deliberately by crying. A sensitive parent can tell when this is happening (the child really wants nothing when the parent arrives, cries without tears, or turns the tears on or off instantly).

It would seem that some degree of self-demand feeding is appropriate, and parents should understand that feeding requirements change over age, vary for different infants, and differ as a function of breast versus bottle feeding, the amount of solids in the diet, and a variety of other factors.

Thumb Sucking and Pacifiers

Another issue that often evokes strong feelings and opinions from parents and experts alike concerns nonnutritive sucking—thumb sucking and the use of pacifiers. To many parents, the sight of a pacifier dangling on a string around a child's neck is revolting. Some grandmothers remember when they were advised that thumb sucking would produce buck teeth (it rarely does because most children stop before permanent teeth emerge). In contrast, both parents and scientists have found that many infants do want to suck on something that does not produce milk, and this apparently does indeed pacify them. One study showed newborn infants to be remarkably calm during circumcision if they were allowed to suck on a pacifier during the operation.

The need to suck. Scholars have debated the issue from another perspective. Freud and his followers (including Benjamin Spock) believe that not only do infants instinctually know how to suck but they have an inborn need to suck. According to this view, infants must do a certain amount of sucking, and if feeding does not provide sufficient opportunity to exhaust sucking needs, then they will turn to their thumbs or pacifiers as alternatives.

The opposing view is that, although the infant is instinctually disposed toward sucking and fundamentally "knows" how to suck at birth, there is no instinctual need to suck for a certain amount of time. Infants who suck thumbs and pacifiers a great deal have learned to do so. Therefore, in contrast to the instinct theory, the learning orientation suggests that if infants were somehow fed by means other than sucking, they would never learn to need to suck and consequently would not suck thumbs or pacifiers.

The evidence. Research on the question is not conclusive, but it leans toward the learning interpretation—with some qualifications. Do all babies suck their thumbs and use pacifiers? In one survey, almost all the babies occasionally sucked some part of the hand, thumb, finger, or whole fist. However, only 44–64 percent were regarded as "thumb suckers." Typically, children who suck a thumb or pacifier start this habit before three months of age. It is less certain when they will stop, with estimates ranging from nine months to more than seven years of age. Approximately half the infants stop by their fourth birthday.

Thumb sucking may begin in ways unrelated to the feeding situation. Some infants come into the world having already practiced thumb sucking in the womb, as

Lennart Nilsson's striking microphotographs have shown. Infants may also learn to suck their thumbs more or less by accident. For example, infants are typically put to sleep lying on their stomachs with their head turned toward one side. Usually, the arms are extended outward at the shoulder and flexed upward at the elbow. In this position the hand lies very near the infant's mouth and can occasionally rub against the lips or cheeks. This stimulation around the mouth triggers off the "rooting reflex" in which touching the infant around the mouth automatically provokes an attempt to suck the stimulating object. Thus some infants may learn to suck their thumbs as a fortuitous consequence of how they are put to bed plus an inborn reflex that otherwise helps them to eat.

But the most crucial test of the instinct versus learning theory has involved attempting to rear some infants on a special cup. The instinct theory predicts that cup-reared infants should have their sucking needs frustrated and should therefore suck their thumbs or other objects more than infants allowed to feed at the breast or bottle. The learning theory predicts that cup-reared infants should suck their thumbs and other objects less because they have not had the opportunity to learn to suck. The results of experiments that tested these predictions have generally favored the learning interpretation.

Sleeping

Newborn infants sleep a great deal. To many exhausted parents, this fact is a godsend. On the average, newborns sleep from 14 to 16 hours a day, or approximately 60–70 percent of the time. Typically, they sleep 3½ hours out of each 4, and rarely go longer than 4½ hours before waking. By six weeks of age, infants sleep only two to four times per day, and by six or seven months they begin to sleep through the night and may rest for up to 10 hours at a time. However, great differences distinguish one baby from another—some infants seem to require more sleep than others; some are more fitful and restless during sleep; and some may sleep through the night after only a few months while still others may take much longer to do this.

Dreaming

Many dog owners have observed their pet in the midst of an apparent dream. The animal is quietly asleep, becomes restless, moves its eyes under closed lids, and sometimes barks or yips suddenly and repeatedly. The rapid eye movements have come to signify this type of sleep, which is called "rapid eye movement" or REM sleep.

Do infants dream? Humans display rapid eye movement sleep, too. In adults, 20 percent of sleep is REM, and it is during REM sleep that adults say they dream. The newborn infant spends as much as half of its sleeping hours in REM, and the percentage may be even higher for premature infants.

Do infants also dream during their REM sleep? It will be difficult to ever answer this question because dreaming usually implies a subjective imagery of events, and infants will never be able to tell us what they "see" when they dream (if they do). But to a neurophysiologist, the eye movements and brain-wave patterns that accompany adult dreaming look very similar to the REM sleep of newborns. Moreover, studies have shown that adults become irritable if deprived of the opportunity to dream, and infants respond similarly if their REM sleep is constantly interrupted.

Dreams about what? Perhaps the most fascinating question is what would a newborn dream about? Adults dream of the past and recombine remembered objects, people, and events into new configurations not previously experienced in reality. It is hard to imagine what

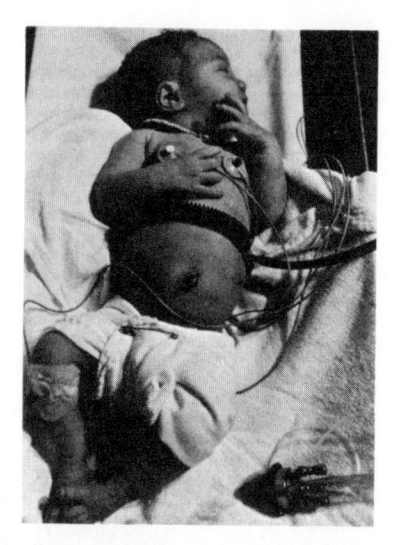

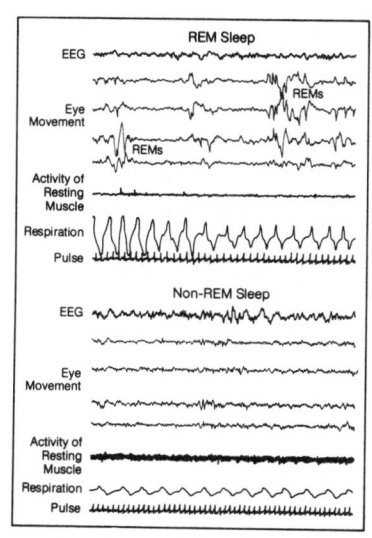

The stabilimeter crib measures the infant's respiration, heartbeat, and eye movements during sleep. Readings show that REM sleep is very different from non-REM sleep because eye activity is greater, respiration is faster, and muscle activity is absent.

a one-day-old infant would "experience" in a dream. Moreover, why is it that the percentage of REM sleep increases with the degree of prematurity of the infant at birth. Why should exceedingly immature infants, ones with presumably less of the experience of which dreams are made, spend nearly all of their sleeping time in REM sleep?

Of course, we do not have conclusive answers to these questions. Drs. H. P. Roffwarg, J. N. Muzil, and W. C. Dement, American experts in sleep research, speculate that REM sleep, especially in infants and prematures, is actually spontaneous neurological firing in the brain that serves a function similar to the idling of an automobile engine. They suspect that some idling or self-generated neurological stimulation is necessary for development and serves to keep the brain at some minimum state of readiness. According to this theory, the developing brain of the fetus is exercised before birth by such random firings and these firings promote its development. If the newborn infant experiences anything during such a "dream," it may be simply random light and sound patterns. As the infant's experience enlarges, the neurological idling may become organized about memories of experiences, and dreaming becomes a more meaningful experience. But no one knows for sure.

Reflexes

Not only do infants arrive with some inborn abilities, nature also ensures the survival and adaptability of children by equipping them with certain reflexes—specific, wired-in responses to particular stimuli. We are probably most familiar with the dilation and constriction of the pupil of the eye to changing light levels and the leg jerk in response to a physician's light hammer tap to the knee.

Infants possess a whole host of reflexes, although many of them are seen more clearly after a few weeks of life. Some of these reflexes are adaptive and help infants to secure food and protect them from harm. Other reflexes are vestiges of man's evolutionary past and no longer serve the adaptive functions they once did. Still, other reflexes are simply signs that certain neurological wiring required for later behaviors is ready several months before it is needed.

ADAPTIVE REFLEXES

One of the most obvious adaptive reflexes is the rooting reflex described briefly above. It is most readily elicited in infants who are one or two weeks old and in a quietly awake state. Parents can see it by laying the infant down on a flat surface, folding the arms over the chest, and gently touching a finger to the corner of the mouth and pulling it slowly toward the cheek. Typically, the infant will move tongue, mouth, and even the entire

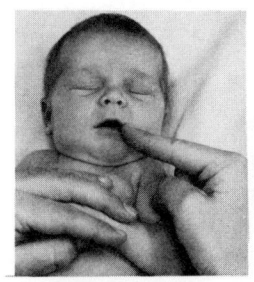

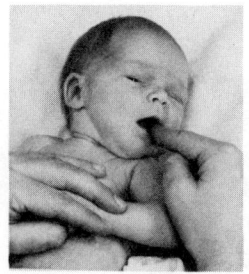

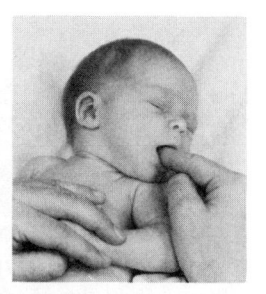

The rooting reflex can be triggered by touching the infant around the mouth—the infant turns toward the finger and grasps it.

head toward the stimulated side and attempt to suck the finger. This reflex is obviously important in feeding, and it seems to be stronger when the infant is hungry. Mothers who breast-feed can observe how the reflex serves this function. Some infants release the nipple for a brief period, only to regain it later. It is easier to retrieve the nipple if it rubs against the side of the mouth and the rooting reflex takes over.

VESTIGES

Another well-known reflex, the "Moro," may be a relic left over from our ancestors, the great apes. If the infant of a few weeks old is held in mid-air and then suddenly dropped down about 15 cm (6 inches), the infant will throw arms upward and close the fingers as shown. This reflex is very adaptive among infant monkeys who are often held by the mother next to her chest or stomach. When the mother moves, the infant monkey's detection of loss of support automatically produces grasping of the mother and hanging on for dear life. No one knows for sure whether the Moro reflex is indeed a vestige of our primate ancestors, but it is a good guess.

SIGNS OF NEUROLOGICAL WIRING

A third set of reflexes reveals the presence of neurological wiring in the first weeks of life that will be

46   The World of the Newborn

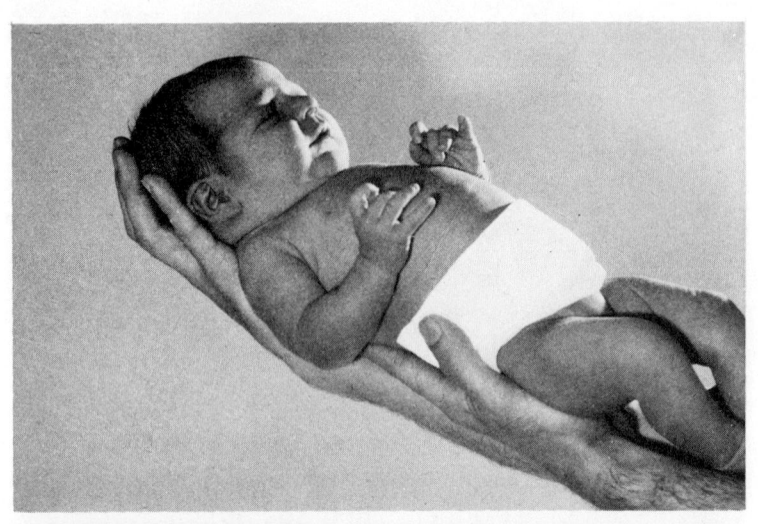

Babies exhibit the Moro reflex when they are dropped suddenly about six inches in space. They throw their arms upward and close their fingers.

used later for important abilities—for example, standing and walking.

If an infant is held carefully, with the head supported, and gently lowered to a table top until the feet

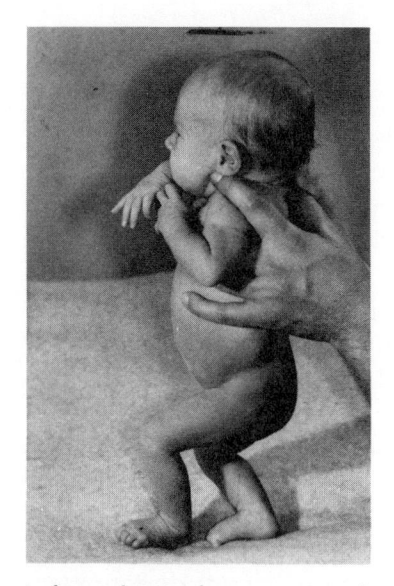

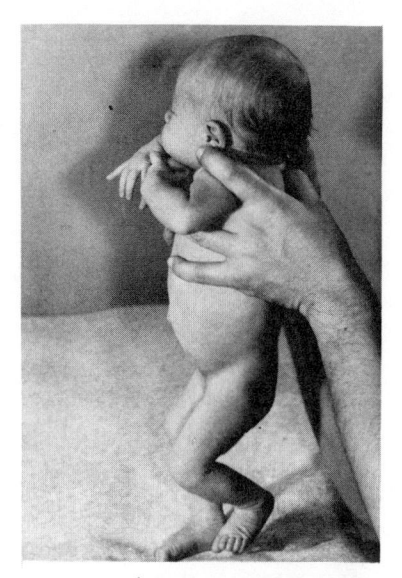

Infants know how to stand even before they are physically capable of doing so, as this baby proves when lowered carefully to a flat surface.

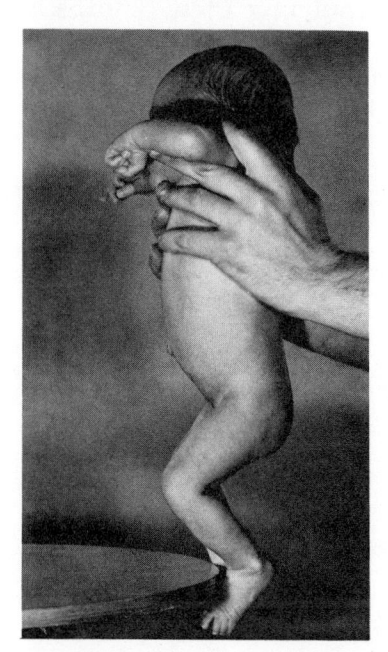

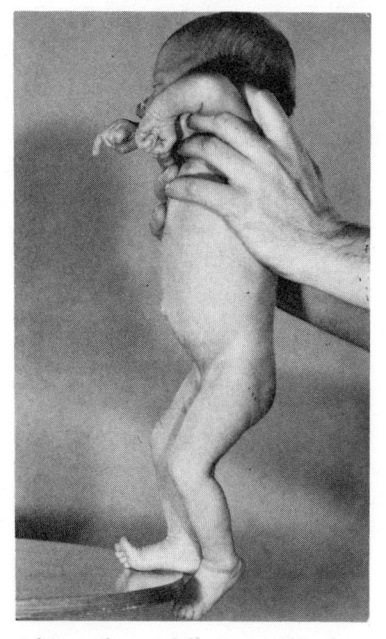

If infants are placed near the edge of a table or with feet gently dragging, they may actually make stepping motions.

touch and knees bend, the legs may straighten as if to stand, especially if the infant is bounced slightly. Of course, the infant is top-heavy and incapable of balancing on those little legs, but the neurological wiring for standing is clearly present. Further, if the infant is leaned forward with feet gently dragging on the table, a steplike movement may occur. This is more obvious if the infant's feet are brought against the edge of the table.

These and many other reflexes are used by pediatricians as a check on the neurological health of newborn infants. Parents should know that even very healthy infants do not always display a reflex every time they are stimulated; whether a reflex action occurs depends on the age of the infant and whether it is quiet or crying, and even skilled and experienced physicians cannot always elicit a reflex at will. Stimulating a few reflexes is a good way for parents to play with their infants, but the use of reflexes as a diagnostic tool is best left in the hands of a pediatric neurologist.

Chapter Four
Preparation for Love and Attachment

NEWBORNS are not only capable of surviving physically in the environment outside the womb; they also are ready to develop social relationships with their caregivers. In short, they are prepared to love and be loved. But infants are not alone in their predisposition toward this special attachment. Parents are ready too. As social partners, infants are remarkably different from adults. Yet, despite the fact that the rules of infant social behavior may be contrary to those typically guiding adult social interactions, most parents seem to know quite naturally how to communicate with infants. In large measure, the pattern of early infancy is like a carefully choreographed dance of parent and infant actions and reactions that helps both partners become acquainted on a common social ground.

The Infant's Capabilities

In 1890, William James said that to an infant the world must be a "blooming, buzzing confusion." Presumably, the newborn is literally assailed by lights, colors, forms, sounds, smells, tastes, and feelings, and because the infant has essentially no experience or methods of interpreting these events, the world must be chaotic and threatening. But newborn infants usually don't look as if they are under attack by their environment. We also know from research that they possess the means for limiting the sensory information that gets through to them, and they are highly selective about what captures and holds their attention. Significantly, the sights and sounds of another person seem especially fascinating to the young infant.

SEEING

Newborns spend most of their time with their eyes closed. This is at least one way in which nature minimizes the buzzing confusion of the new world. But we

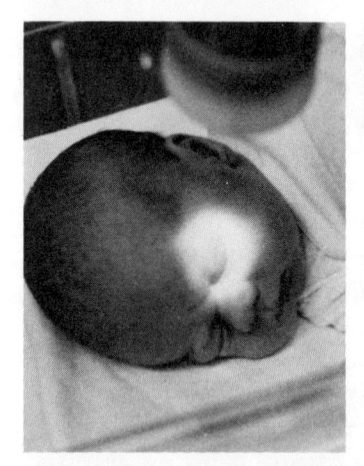

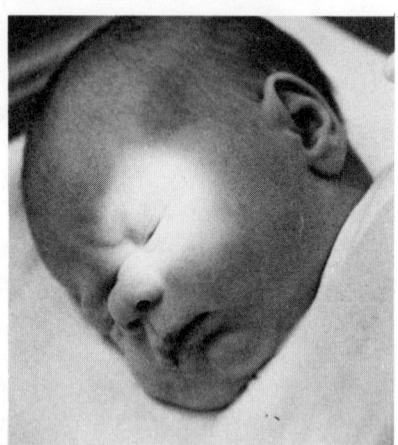

Babies prefer dim or moderate levels of light. They tend to turn away from brightness or to tighten up their eyelids and fuss.

should not assume from this that newborns cannot see. In fact they see fairly well, but in a limited way.

Brightness. Newborns certainly detect light, and they are quite sensitive to bright lights, perhaps because the pigmentation of the iris of their eyes is not fully developed at birth. Therefore lights that are bright to adults will be still brighter to infants. If given a choice, newborns prefer what adults would consider dim to moderate levels of light. Parents no doubt have observed this sensitivity to light. When infants are quietly resting, even lightly sleeping, and are then moved into the sunlight for a moment, they may tighten their eyelids and fuss in the light, relaxing again when they are returned to the shadows.

Clarity. It is one thing to detect light, especially bright light; it is another thing to see pattern and form. How clearly can newborns see objects in their environment—their caregivers, for example?

Normal seeing adults are said to have 20/20 vision. In contrast, newborn infants have approximately 20/500 vision, which means that objects they see clearly at a distance of 6 meters (20 feet), the standard adult can see just as sharply at a distance of 152 meters (500 feet). In some sense, adults see objects twenty-five times better than newborn infants. By this reckoning, it seems that newborns are essentially blind. From one standpoint, they are. Newborns could not see a tree trunk with diameter of 30.5 cm (12 inches) if it were more than 42 meters (46 yards) away. While objects that are distant from the infant are seen in only fuzzy relief, up close the world seems a little clearer. Newborns can see a human finger at less than 2.8 meters (9 feet), the iris of a parent's eye at 1.4 meters (4½ feet), the pupil of the eye at 41.5 cm (16.5 inches), and a medium-sized freckle at 27.8 cm (11 inches). So newborns can clearly see most features of the human face at about 18–38 cm (7–15 inches).

But these statements are very approximate because the ability of the lens of the eye to focus on an object is only one of many factors that determine how clearly we see something. For example, infants are much less sensitive than adults to the difference in brightness between the light and dark areas in what we see. Objects are less distinct to an infant not only because they are out of focus, but because they do not stand out so well from the background of other objects. Objects that are up close are seen better primarily because they are bigger, better illuminated, and have sharper contrast than objects that are farther away. Thus objects, including a parent's face, are seen best if they are within approximately 18–38 cm (7–15 inches) of the infant's eyes.

As the weeks pass, visual acuity improves rapidly. By two months of age, infants have approximately 20/200 vision. Though this is the definition of legal blindness in some American states, the infant can now see the iris of the eye of an adult in the same room (within 3.4 meters

How well can babies see? These photographs simulate the infant's vision of a landscape and a mother's face at the newborn, two-month, and six-month stages.

or 11.3 feet) and the pupil of the eye if the person is within a meter (40 inches). By six months of age, infants see about as clearly as adults do (20/20).

The implications of this early inability to see objects clearly are staggering. Most objects in the visual world of the newborn are too fuzzy to be seen. In this way nature once again shields babies from much stimulation. To sense this for yourself, place the tip of your thumb on your nose and extend your little finger as far away from your face as possible. Now focus your eyes on your little fingernail, but simultaneously direct your attention to objects elsewhere in the room. Move your head around and you will get some impression of the psychedelic light show that constitutes background to the infant's visual world. To be sure, you can identify objects across the room, but remember that your experience with those objects permits you to fill in absent sensory information and recognize the object even when you don't see it very clearly.

Lacking this skill, newborn infants have a very limited meaningful visual world, and few objects are seen clearly because they are too far away. But something that often does come close—and will be in focus—is the face of the infant's caregiver. This may be a way nature helps parent and child to become important to one another.

Colors. Do newborns perceive color? If they do not, then all those fancy colors on mobiles and toys are lost on the infant, if not on the adult who buys them. This had been a surprisingly difficult question for scientists to answer for a variety of technical reasons, but it now appears that infants do see colors and they may even see them in the same way adults do.

THE RULES OF LOOKING

Infants do not simply stare into space, hoping an interesting object will zip by close enough for them to see it clearly. They have certain strategies of scanning the world around them, and some objects seem more interesting than others. Much of what we know about how newborns search the visual world and what they look at is due to the creative research of three psychologists, Drs. William Kessen at Yale University, Marshall Haith at the University of Denver, and Phillip Salapatek at the Institute of Child Development, University of Minnesota.

Suppose a newborn wakes up in a totally dark room. The eyes are likely to open and search for light. This scanning consists of short eye movements, predominantly horizontal rather than vertical, executed with a certain rhythm—approximately two scans per second, or roughly the same rate as the infant's speed of sucking. If the room is suddenly illuminated, the infant will search for "edges of brightness." Since scanning is likely to be horizontal, vertical stripes or edges, especially ones that have high contrast (black against white), are most likely to be detected by this horizontal scanning strategy. In fact, the infant attends mostly to the points of highest contrast, which are often the edges and corners of objects. Once found, the newborn tends to stare at those points of high contrast rather than systematically examine the entire object.

When a parent bends over a quietly awake infant, what does the baby look at? Typically, the movement of the parent's face as it enters the infant's visual field will promote scanning by the newborn. In the course of this horizontal searching, the most likely "edge" the infant will encounter is the hairline at the top or side of the face, especially as it contrasts with the background (often a white ceiling or wall). The result is sometimes disconcerting to new parents who want to have eye-to-eye contact with their infant, but must "chase" their infant's eyes before being able to look directly into them.

By six to ten weeks of age, the infant is more skillful. Now, rather than concentrating on the outside edges of a parent's face, the infant will scan high-contrast areas within the general facial outline—mainly the eyes, nose, and mouth. In fact, by two to three months of age, if the parent talks face-to-face with the infant, the child now seems to locate the parent's eyes rather quickly. This is a remarkable event, because infants of this age usually look at objects that make sounds. One would think they should look at a speaking parent's mouth, not the eyes. Not so—there is something special about a talking person that is different from a noisy object. Just why the rules should be different for face-to-face speech is not clear; but it is a happy contradiction because eye-to-eye contact is a vital component of early social relations, feelings of intimacy, and attachment.

Hearing

Newborn infants hear fairly well. Actually the cochlea, the main hearing organ in the inner ear, is operating four months before birth; the basic neurological wiring that enables the infant to discriminate between different tones and intensities is probably available two months before birth; and the infant is prepared to direct attention toward sounds approximately one month before birth. The newborn's ability to detect a sound is almost as good as the average adult's, but skill in distinguishing one sound from another is far less advanced. Apparently newborns can notice the difference between tones of 200 and 1000 cycles per second, which is roughly comparable to the difference between a fog horn and a clarinet. However, some newborns can respond to differences of only one step on the musical scale. Therefore infants can certainly hear their caregivers talk to them, although speech may sound more like a monotone.

Response to human speech. As George Orwell put it in *Animal Farm,* some sounds are more equal than others as far as a newborn is concerned. In fact, human speech seems to be very special, so special that it is fair to conclude that newborns are highly disposed to listening to as well as to seeing their caregivers.

If pure tones of different frequencies or pitch are played to an infant, what can we observe? Research by Drs. Rita Eisenberg at St. Joseph Hospital in Lancaster, Pennsylvania, and John Hutt at the University of Keele in England has demonstrated that infants respond best to sounds in the range of the human voice. They are most responsive to the higher pitches when awake, but to lower pitches when drowsy. Lower tones will calm infants who are upset, while higher notes may arouse or even stress babies. Perhaps this is why fathers, whose voices are lower, sometimes can calm an infant more quickly than mothers. Moreover, if fluctuating tones of various lengths are played to infants, a sequence lasting from 5 to 15 seconds before a pause seems to produce more response in a resting infant than tone sequences lasting for shorter or longer durations.

With these observations in mind, consider how adults talk to infants. First, they tend to speak to infants in unusually high-pitched voices. Second, their short sentences are repetitive, and a bout of conversation tends to last roughly 5 to 15 seconds before a pause. Somehow adults are naturally disposed to talking to babies at a tonal frequency and temporal pace to which the newborn is most attentive and responsive.

Although it is not obvious to us, adults perceive certain speech sounds in distinct categories. With modern electronic equipment, it is possible to produce sounds artificially that are very close to adult speech. For example, one can electronically create syllables similar to *pah* or *bah*. The advantage of artificial sound production is that syllables in the range between *pah* and *bah* can be produced quite accurately. When adults are played these intermediate sounds, however, they do not hear them as halfway between *pah* and *bah* but either as *pah* or *bah*.

Dr. Peter Eimas and his colleagues at Brown University found that infants apparently hear in the same way that adults do in this regard: graded sounds are heard either as *pah* or *bah*, not halfway between, and the *pah* and *bah* categories encompass precisely the same sounds as they do for adults. This observation provokes speculation that there is an inherent association between human speech and human hearing. Not only is the human ear maximally tuned to the human voice, but we hear different sounds in the same way that we speak them. And much of this ability may be available to the newborn. If so, speech may not be a buzzing confusion for the newborn. Infants may hear speech sounds much as we hear it right from the start.

Moreover, with a little practice, infants also learn to recognize their caregiver's voice. Dr. Margaret Mills of the University of London found that infants between twenty and thirty days of age would suck on a nipple more if such sucking resulted in their hearing a tape recording of their own mother's voice rather than a strange woman's conversation.

Dancing to human speech. A conversation is more than speaking and listening. As adults, we comprehend words, sentences, and train of thought, and then we respond, perhaps by agreeing or disagreeing with the speaker. But adults also respond in far more subtle ways to human speech, ways that require fine-grained photography to discern.

Dr. William Condon of Boston University School of Medicine has observed that adults actually change their casual, restless, almost random movements in rhythm with changes in the syllabic content of the speech to which they are listening. Suppose three or four adults are standing in a corner at a cocktail party, and one is describing her trip to Scandinavia. The listeners may adjust their fingers on their glasses, shift weight from one leg to the other, flex a leg, arm, or finger during the course of the conversation. Careful analysis of these movements of listeners indicates that changes from movement to nonmovement or shifts in the direction of movements are timed to coincide with the end of one syllable and the beginning of the next in the speaker's monologue. Which movements occur is largely irrelevant; the important point is that whatever movements do occur, they are made just when the speaker changes from one syllable to the next.

In an intriguing but still controversial study conducted with Dr. Louis W. Sander, Condon has suggested that newborn infants may also synchronize their movement patterns with adult speech. Moreover, it appears that it is definitely human speech that provokes this interaction—which amounts to a subtle ballet. If pure tones are presented at approximately the same rate as human speech, synchronization of infant movement with sound changes does not seem to occur. Moreover, babies of English-speaking parents move in concert with both English and Chinese speech. But if the speaker simply babbles disconnected vowel sounds without the natural rhythm of normal speech, the newborn stops matching movement with phonetic pattern.

This early social behavior is quite remarkable. The human face embodies stimulating characteristics to which the infant is maximally attentive, probably not because it is a face but because it has sharp contours and points of high contrast. In addition, parents and caregivers are likely to talk to newborn infants in unique ways that match the sensitivity of the infant to the frequency, utterance length, tonal pattern, and rhythm of such speech. An adult speaking softly to a newborn infant who is being held in close range is almost an ideal stimulus for the infant.

SMELL

Drs. Trig Engen, Louis Lipsitt, and Herbert Kaye at Brown University observed that newborn infants could distinguish between pairs of smells chosen from anise oil (licorice), asafetida (garlic), acetic acid (vinegar), and phenyl alcohol. With repeated exposures to a given smell, the infants gradually came to take no notice of it, but when a new smell was suddenly introduced, they detected the difference. Therefore, infants are clearly able to smell some odors, to learn and remember that they have previously encountered a given smell, and to notice the difference between one odor and another.

But the substances used in this experiment were strong-smelling indeed. Can the infant recognize its own mother by smell? Dr. Aidan Macfarlane in Oxford asked nursing mothers to wear gauze pads inside their bras between feedings. Then the mother's pad was

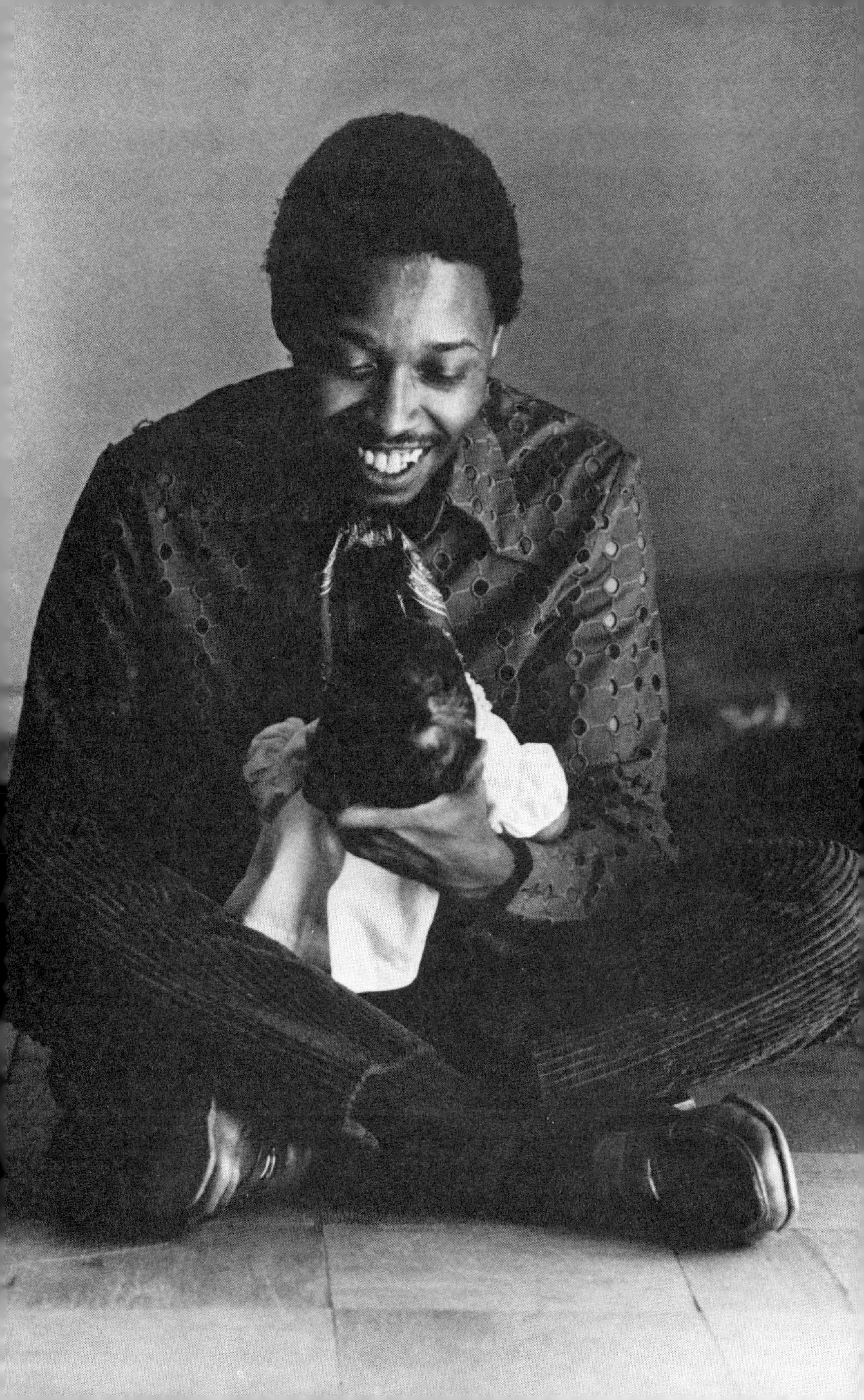

placed near one side of her baby's face while a clean pad was located on the other side. Even infants of only five days of age tended to turn their heads to their mother's pad rather than to the clean pad, apparently recognizing special smells associated with feeding.

In another study, Macfarlane compared pads worn by the newborn's mother with those worn by another mother. At two days of age, the infants did not seem to be able to tell the difference, but by six days of age they spent more time facing their mother's pad than that of the strange mother, and at ten days the difference was even more striking.

Macfarlane conducted yet another study to determine whether the week-old infants were smelling their mother or their mother's milk. The result seemed to support the conclusion that it is the smell of the mother, more than her milk, that allows the infant to recognize her in this way. (Parenthetically, when Macfarlane told the mothers that these studies were being conducted to determine if their babies could smell them, many wanted to splash on deodorant, which not only would have ruined the experiment but also spoiled nature's plan to bring infant and parent together.)

Taste

Much of our sense of taste is really based upon smell, as we discover when a head cold clogs our nose and food doesn't seem to have much flavor. Is the newborn's ability to taste good enough to detect differences in fluids even when those fluids smell the same? Lipsitt and his colleagues at Brown University determined that newborns would suck at different speeds for different levels of sweetness in similar-smelling fluids they were being fed. Moreover, Dr. David Salisbury at Oxford University found that breathing, sucking, and swallowing patterns are different when infants are fed by formula than when they are fed by breast milk. Thus it seems reasonable to suppose that newborns detect differences in taste even when the smell is the same, and they may taste the difference between formula and breast milk (although we do not know which tastes better).

The Parents' Role

We have seen that the infant's senses and perceptual systems are tailored to fit stimuli provided by the caregivers. In return, adults may also be disposed toward babies in ways that facilitate relationships and attachments. Because adults are more flexible and capable, of course, they have a greater responsibility to change their behavior to fit the infant's perceptual and physical abilities. For example, we have seen that adults raise their voices and speak in shorter, more repetitive sentences when talking to babies. But there are many other ways that adults prepare to meet infants on a common ground.

THE APPEAL OF BABIES

The sight of a baby is a powerful stimulus for many people. New parents often discover this when they take their infant out for a stroll or shopping trip. If the infant's face is visible to passersby, complete strangers invariably smile and some come up to gush at the infant in the most ridiculous manner.

Babyishness. What causes them to do this? One suggestion is that the sheer sight of an infant's face, and perhaps to a lesser extent the entire body of an infant, automatically releases warm, protective, friendly behavior from adults. This notion was first introduced by the ethologist Konrad Lorenz and more recently reemphasized by Irenäus Eibl-Eibesfeldt of The Max-Planck Institute for behavioral physiology.

It has been known for many years that animals respond instinctively to certain stimuli. A very famous example comes from Lorenz: young ducklings followed him in a row shortly after hatching. The sight of a mov-

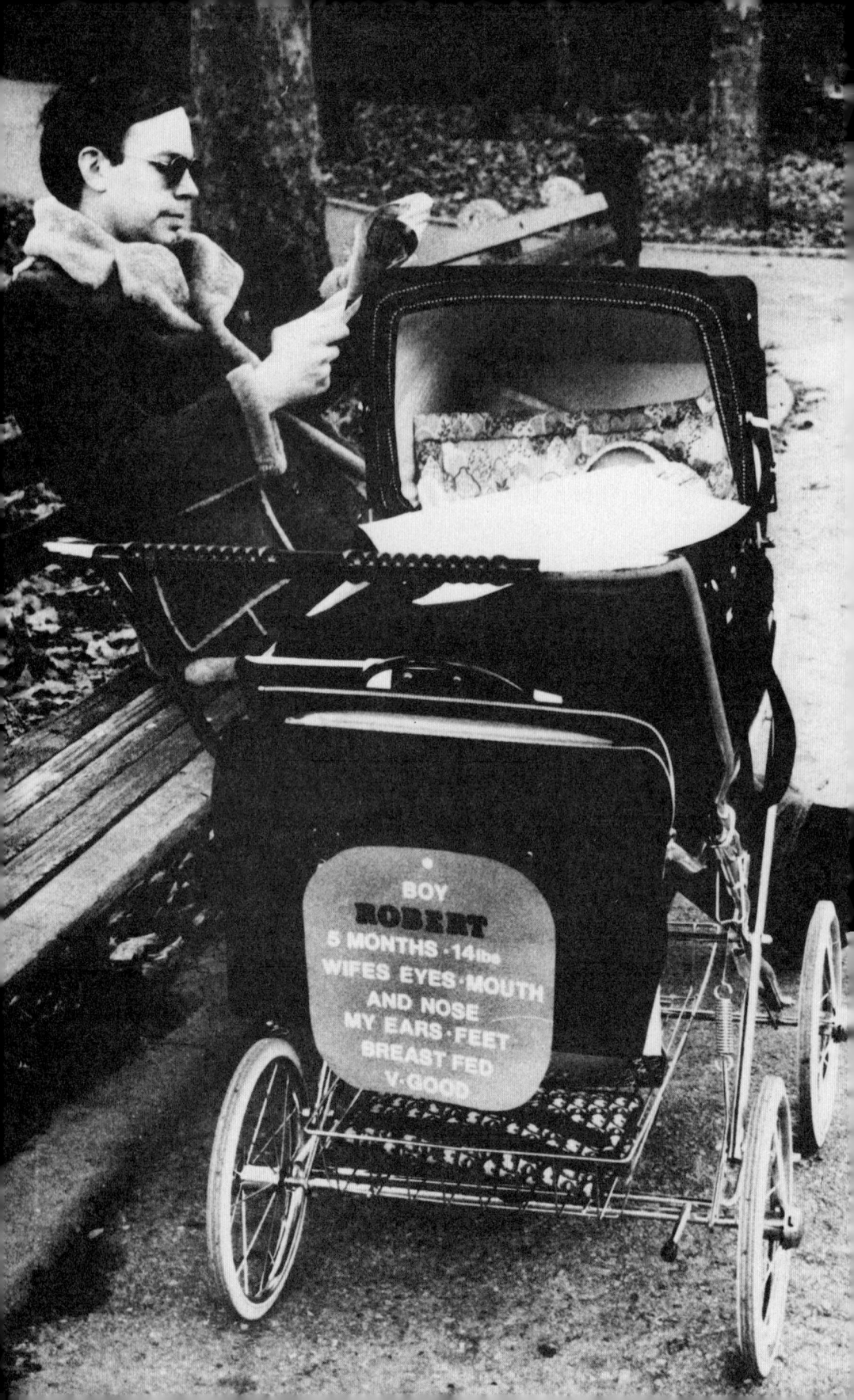

BOY
ROBERT
5 MONTHS · 14lbs
WIFES EYES · MOUTH
AND NOSE
MY EARS · FEET
BREAST FED
V· GOOD

These baby geese trailed after Konrad Lorenz as if he were their mother because they saw him—and not their real mother— hours after hatching.

What constitutes "babyishness"? A comparison of the visual features of four species—human, rabbit, dog, and bird—reveals that the relationship of baby to adult size and proportions is similar. In each case the infant characteristics, but not the adult ones, elicit parental responses.

ing object at that time in development "released" this behavior. But Lorenz also asked the reverse question: Could affectionate adult behavior be automatically stimulated by the sight of an infant?

The notion is both intriguing and plausible. Lorenz noticed that the faces of the young look different from corresponding adults in essentially the same way across a variety of animal species. Infants tend to have a larger head in proportion to the size of the body, a larger and

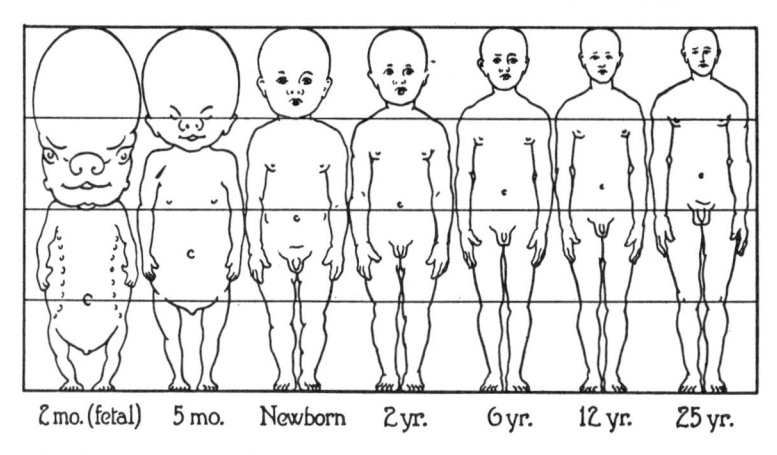

The human body changes dramatically in form and proportion in the period from fetal to adult life.

more protruding forehead relative to the remainder of the face, oversized eyes positioned lower on the face, round protruding cheeks, and a relatively flat versus pointed nose or snout. Presumably, these are the characteristics of babies that promote special responses from adults.

There is some evidence that this is true. Adults report that they like pictures of young animals and humans more than pictures of mature members of those species. Moreover, they prefer caricatures in which the features typical of infants are accentuated. Such affinity for babies seems to increase markedly in girls at approximately twelve to fourteen years of age and in boys about two years later, approximately the ages of puberty. However, the tendency to respond in special ways to infants may even be present much earlier: parents often state that there is nothing like another baby to excite their own. Moreover, some studies suggest that infants between four and twenty months tend to look differently at pictures of babies than at pictures of older children or adults—but it is not known whether these infants actually prefer the pictures of infants.

In addition to their looks, babies behave in special ways that also seem to elicit positive, affectionate behavior from adults. Dr. Daniel Stern of the Cornell University Medical Center has spent a good deal of time observing and videotaping parents and their infants. He reports that when infants smile, widen their eyes, and open their mouths while throwing their heads back and thrusting out their tongues, adults consistently smile and respond affectionately. The opening of the mouth is particularly effective.

Instant love? While the two- to four-month-old infant is almost always attractive to someone, babies are not so beautiful when parents first see them moments after delivery. They have been described as squinting, cross-eyed, potbellied, bowlegged, with shriveled skin and a deafening, dismal cry. Others have likened the physical appearance of the newborn to a badly defeated prizefighter—swollen eyelids, puffy bruised skin, a broad nose flattened across the face, and ears matted back at weird angles.

The newborn emerges blotched with the mother's blood and covered with a whitish greasy material called the vernix, which has served as a lubricant for the passage through the birth canal. The puffed, wrinkled appearance derives in part from the presence of fluid and small pads of fat under the skin which will help nutritionally to tide the infant over until the first meal. Some

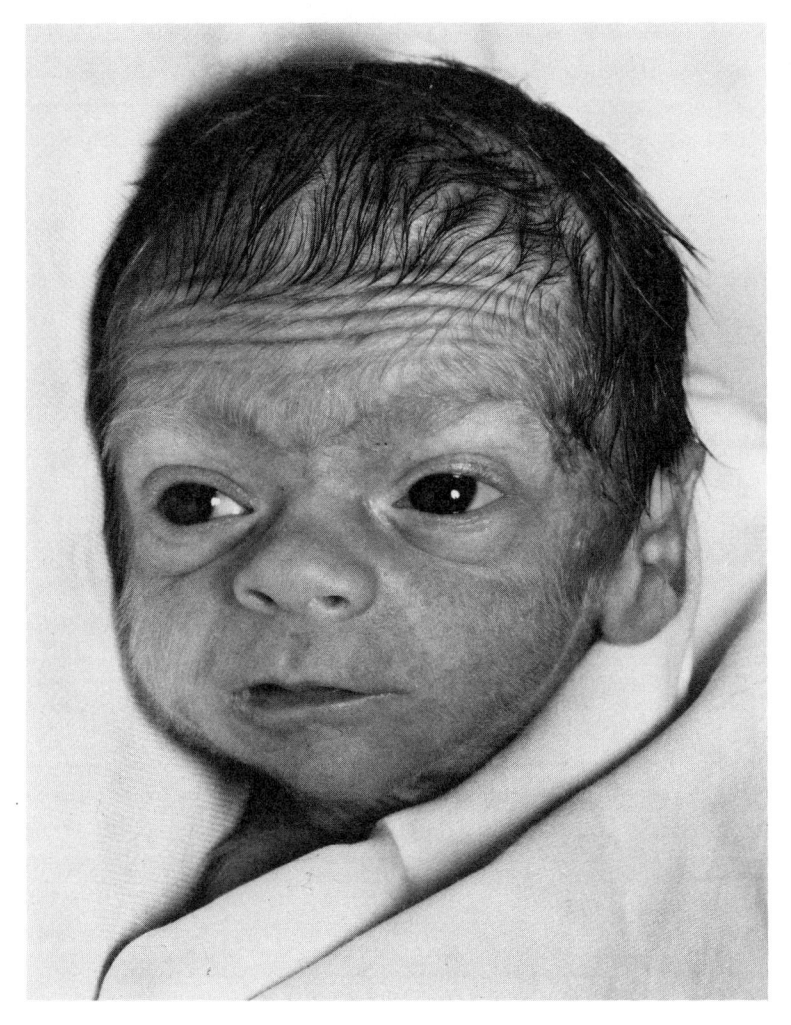

Just after delivery, babies are not overly attractive. This normal premature baby is typical of newborns in terms of facial hair and feature proportions.

newborns have considerable downy body hair, called lanugo, which may initially appear pasted to the skin by the vernix, and after cleaning and drying some of them look quite furry for awhile.

The battered or lopsided appearance of the head is

produced in part by the fact that the skull "bones" are not yet hard. Actually they are overlapping pieces of cartilage and not mature bones at all. This gives the infant a smaller head, which can pass more easily through the mother's pelvis, and it allows for substantial growth as these plates move apart and eventually become knit together to form a solid skull. However, the aesthetic price for this mechanical advantage is that the newborn's head appears rather lumpy, and soft areas, called the fontanels, may pulsate up and down as blood is pumped about the head. At the other end of the body, the legs are often bowed and the feet may be pigeon-toed or even cocked at strange angles, all because of the cramped quarters of the womb.

If parents are expecting to see an infant resembling those pictured on baby products and magazine covers, they may be utterly shocked by the sight of their newborn and feel guilty because they do not immediately love their baby. Aidan Macfarlane asked 97 mothers of two-month infants when they first felt love for their babies. Forty-one percent said it was during pregnancy, 24 percent said at birth, 27 percent said during the first week, and 8 percent said they did not experience love until later. Moreover, only 31 percent said their love increased at birth, whereas 40 percent remembered an increase of affection during the first two weeks after birth. In studies conducted by Drs. Howard Moss and Kenneth Robson at the National Institute of Mental Health, many women revealed feelings of strangeness and unfamiliarity toward their newborn infants, feelings that persisted for the first few weeks of life. Some mothers experience "instant love," but not all, and many feel their affection grows in the weeks following birth.

Infant abuse. Although babyish looks and actions are endearing to many adults, they are not sufficient to bring out the best caregiving behavior in everyone.

Parental love is not a universal instinct. A few societies in the world do not treat their infants with warmth and affection. A small tribe on the northern border of Uganda known as the Ik developed a ruthless strategy toward life in the wake of a struggle to survive famine, and the attitude lingered on even in better circumstances. Children are regarded as useless appendages, and if an infant or toddler is hurt or carried off by a predator, the parent feels relieved rather than grieved at the loss. After the age of three, children are turned out on their own.

Societies like the Ik are rare but not unique. Anthropologist Margaret Mead described the more prosperous Mundugumor people of New Guinea as having no such instinct as mother love. Many infants are killed, and those allowed to survive are treated with disdain, contempt, and resentment.

Lest those of us living in more "civilized" societies become too smug, consider the alarming rates of child abuse in the United States and Great Britain. It is conservatively estimated that 250,000 children are abused, 100,000 are placed in foster care because their parents have mistreated them, and more than 2000 are actually killed by their parents every year in the United States. In Great Britain approximately 300–600 children are thought to be murdered by their parents every year. These numbers are too high to be considered rare aberrations of human behavior. Clearly, something else besides babyishness is required for parental love.

Communicating and Influencing

Babies in the first few weeks of life do respond to their parents' overtures. They look, smile occasionally, and babble. But at this stage these actions are predominantly reflexive and occur somewhat randomly. In fact, smiles are most frequently seen in light sleep, rather than in the course of play with a caregiver. How, then, do infants and adults socially interact with one another?

Mutual Gazing

The principal vehicle of social interaction for an infant is looking at the caregiver. This is perhaps the only type of communication over which the infant has control. That is, infants can look and, importantly, they can stop looking. Infants cannot turn on or off their hearing or other senses in the way they can open and close their eyes or turn their heads away when they are bored or agitated. Therefore, one of the first true social interactions, involving accommodation and reciprocal communication on the part of both parent and newborn, appears to be simply looking into one another's eyes.

This experience has been filmed and closely studied: a mother waits until the infant is in a state of quiet alertness, with eyes open, and then faces the infant close enough for optimum focusing by the infant. The baby looks at the parent and maintains the interaction by not looking away or closing the eyes as the parent changes facial expressions or speaks. Both partners accommodate to one another, and both are capable of turning on and turning off the interplay. These are requirements for true social relations. Finally, while we do not know if babies find mutual looking pleasurable, parents apparently do because it is common for parents to note that mutual gazing marks the beginning of their feelings of love for their baby.

Early Contact

Special opportunities for skin-to-skin contact between parent and infant during the first few days of life may help the start of attachment between them. Herb Leiderman at Stanford Medical School and Marshall Klaus and John Kennell at Case Western Reserve University School of Medicine have pioneered research on the effects of parent-infant contact in the newborn nursery.

Klaus and Kennell undertook a study to determine if

early contact between mother and infant would increase their attachment. Fourteen mothers of first-born, normal, full-term infants were treated according to standard obstetrical and pediatric practices in major hospitals in the United States. One group of mothers were given a short glimpse of their infant at birth, brief contact at six to eight hours of age, and then visits of twenty to thirty minutes for feedings every four hours before leaving the hospital when the infant was approximately four days old. A second group of mothers, similar in most respects to the first, were given their naked babies for one hour during the first two hours after delivery and for five extra hours on each of the next three days of the infant's life. Thus they had sixteen more hours of contact with their babies than the other group had.

Klaus and Kennell filmed the behavior of the early-contact mothers with their infants during the first hours of life. It happens that many babies are quite alert for a short period of time after delivery, thus facilitating sensory contact with their mother. Also, radiant heat units were set up for the early-contact pairs so that the infants could be naked. Shortly after birth the infant was placed on the mother's chest and stomach. At first, the mother gingerly touched her delicate infant only with her fingertips. Then she gently moved her fingers over the infant's body, gradually allowing her entire hand to caress the baby. Finally, the mother made careful but deliberate attempts to reposition herself and the infant so that they could look into each other's eyes. The mothers often asked their babies to look at them, especially if the baby became drowsy, and many reported that their mounting excitement reached a crescendo when eye-to-eye contact was finally made.

Mothers and infants in both groups returned to the hospital one month later. Mothers who had experienced early contact soothed their crying babies more during a stressful physical examination, engaged in more eye-to-eye contact and fondling during feeding, and were more

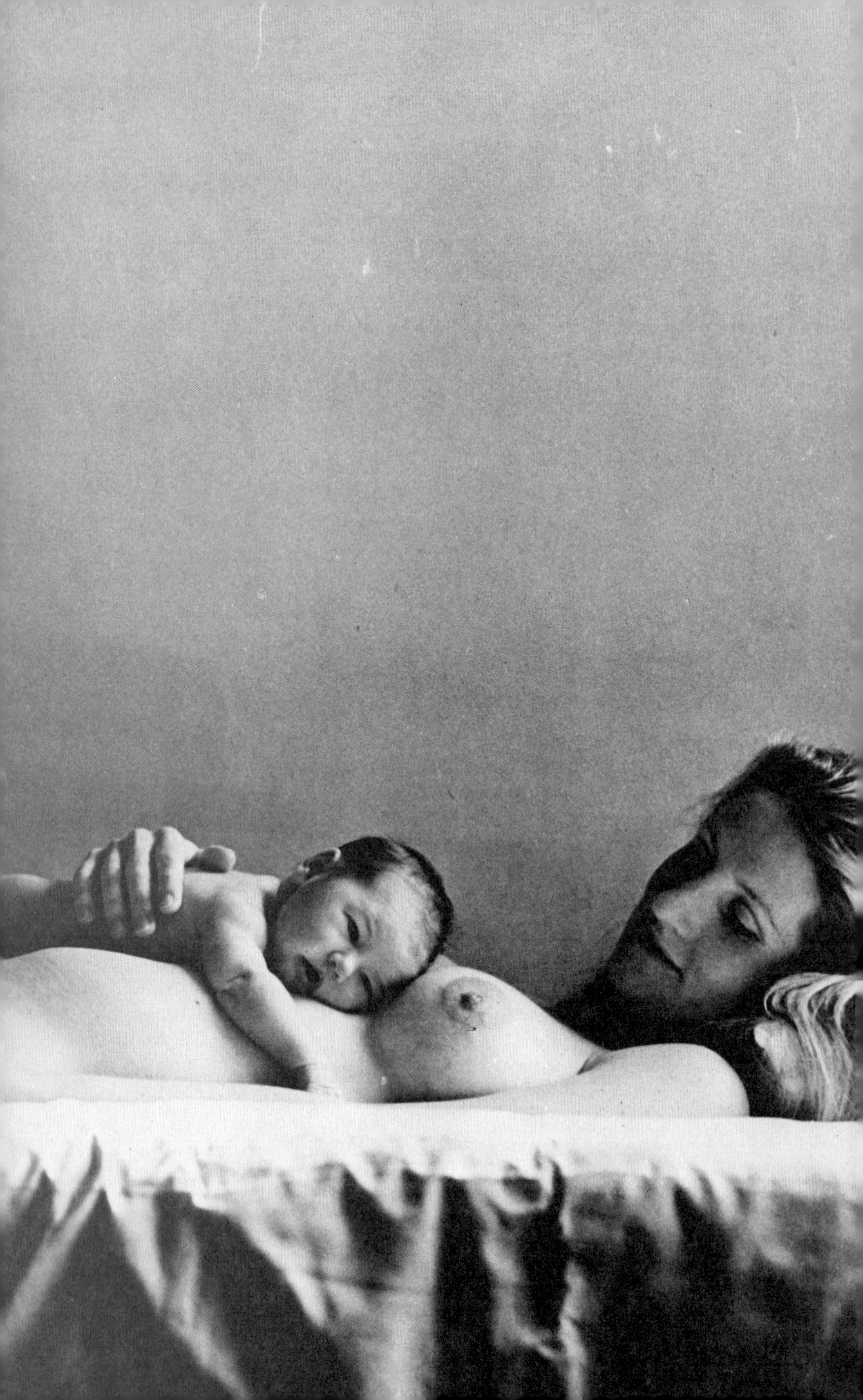

reluctant to leave their infants with strangers than mothers not given the extra-contact experience.

Some of the same mothers and infants were assessed again when the infant was two years old. The early-contact mothers spoke differently to their infants than those who did not have extra contact; they asked twice as many questions and issued fewer commands; and their sentences were longer and contained fewer content words and more adjectives.

Several other researchers have also explored the possible effects of early contact. Some studies conducted in Brazil, Guatemala, and Sweden revealed that early contact was associated with more successful and longer breast feeding. Moreover, Brazilian and Guatemalan babies having early contact experience gained more weight and had fewer infections. The Swedish mothers who had early contact kissed their infants more and engaged in more mutual gazing three months after birth than did mothers who did not have the extra social contact. Their babies also cried less and laughed more than those infants not receiving the special experience.

Early contact may also affect fathers and marriages. In Sweden, fathers who were asked to undress their infant and to establish eye-to-eye contact for one hour during the first three days of life were found to offer more paternal caregiving to their infants three months later. One study at Stanford University found fewer divorces among a small group of parents given special early-contact experience, and two babies in the late-contact group were subsequently given up for adoption. However, this research involved only a few cases, and more study is required before one can firmly conclude that early contact keeps families together.

But not all research on this topic is quite so compelling. In Leiderman's research on mothers of premature babies, the extra-contact mothers displayed greater affection and attachment during the first few days or weeks after birth, but there were no noticeable differences two or three months later. Moreover, even the differences associated with early contact that were observed were smaller than differences associated with the sex of the infant and whether it was a first- or later-born baby. Another study revealed that early contact only influenced mothers of first-born infants; it had no effect if the mother had given birth to other children. These apparent limitations seem to indicate that early contact may be helpful but not necessary for good parenting, for physically and psychologically healthy infants, or for the development of affectionate attachment.

The results of Klaus and Kennell's work have been widely publicized, and many hospitals have changed traditional nursery-room procedures to provide early-contact experiences for mothers and sometimes fathers. Most professionals regard this as a healthy change. However, some people get the wrong impression from this new emphasis and have come to believe that a sound, emotionally fulfilling relationship with an infant is impossible without early contact. Klaus has described this as the "epoxy" belief—it is as if the glue that can bond parent and infant is wet for only a few hours after birth and, unless the two partners get together at that time, the glue will dry and they will never be able to stick together.

No evidence exists to verify the epoxy notion. Early contact may help certain parents get off to a good start, but it is not required for the development of a healthy, secure, loving relationship between parent and baby. Parents denied this experience for a variety of reasons (it was not hospital policy, they adopted their baby, the mother was too tired or sedated) are not forever estranged from their offspring. Nor is early contact alone sufficient to keep parent and child attached forever. Love between two people is the product of a continuing relationship. It cannot be eternally cemented into place by a few hours of contact in the first days of life. That is only a beginning.

Part Three
The First Year

Chapter Five
The Growth of Mentality

HUMANS POSSESS numerous characteristics that distinguish them from other animals. For example, the opposed thumb allows humans to grasp objects with great dexterity and precision, a skill that is instrumental in handling tools. But unquestionably it is the diverse accomplishments of the human mind that grant levels of language and thought far beyond anything known in lower animals. In a word, it is human intelligence that makes us unique.

The Nature of Intelligence

Perhaps no human characteristic has been debated more heatedly in the last few years than intelligence. What is it? Is it inherited? Can it be influenced by experience? Does it change in the course of a lifetime? What are its roots in infancy?

In a sense, everyone knows what intelligence is even though it is difficult to define. Scholars have stated that intelligence is the ability to reason or to think abstractly, to learn or profit from experience, to adapt to one's environment, to solve problems, and to accumulate knowledge and information. All these skills are undoubtedly related to intelligence, and yet a precise definition of the concept escapes us. When we say that Jane Doe is a smart woman, most people know what we mean—somehow we agree on a usable but unstated notion of intelligence. The concept is similar to that of gravity: we all know what it is, but even physicists have a difficult time defining it.

Until recently, whatever its specific character, intelligence was thought to be unitary, pervasive, and constant over age: unitary, because people were thought to possess a single intelligence, as opposed to many different unrelated mental abilities; pervasive, because it was assumed that nearly every aspect of mental behavior was a reflection of that one intelligence; constant, because people observed that individuals are not bright one day and dull the next.

These were not merely dogmatic beliefs; psychological science seemed to support them. When children or adults were given a battery of tests measuring a variety of different mental abilities, people who scored well on one test tended to score well on others. It was as if they possessed a single ability that allowed them to perform more or less competently on a great diversity of mental tasks. Moreover, the Stanford-Binet and Wechsler Intelligence Scales provided an accurate measure of that general mental ability and became known as intelligence tests. In addition, if such tests were administered periodically from early childhood through adulthood, individuals who scored well at one testing tended to score well on a later examination. In fact, individual differences in intelligence test scores were so consistent over age that one scientist proclaimed that adult intelligence is half determined by age four, and three fourths determined by age six. Studies also showed that intelligence ran in families—the more closely related two people are, the more similar are they in IQ. Identical twins are closer to one another than are fraternal twins or ordinary siblings. Presumably, intelligence is influenced by our genes.

These scientific observations are accurate, but the sweeping conclusions are not warranted. First, as research continued, psychologists discovered some forms of creativity that did not obviously relate to scores on an intelligence test. Of course, a certain level of mental competence is required to be creative, but intelligence-test scores do not predict whether mentally normal individuals are creative or not.

Second, while many individuals receive approximately the same score on intelligence tests throughout childhood, many others do not. As described in Chapter 1, studies at the Fels Research Institute, where children were given intelligence tests periodically from two and a half to seventeen years of age, revealed that the average child in the group changed 28.5 IQ points over the course of the study. In fact, one out of three children changed 30 points or more, one out of seven changed 40 points or more, and one person increased 74 IQ points (which is equivalent to rising from the lowest thirteenth percentile to the very top of the population). These changes in IQ over age were not simply random fluctuations in performance; rather, they represented progressive increases or decreases in relative performance. It should be stressed that these were normal children reared in typical middle-class homes, not mistreated individuals locked in rooms and suddenly released. Clearly, intelligence is not unitary, pervasive, or necessarily constant over age, as people thought.

Is it Inherited?

This is a very complicated question. Some scientists believe that close to 70 percent of the difference between people within races and ethnic groups in contemporary industrialized societies is associated with their genetic backgrounds. However, this does not mean that mental performance cannot be changed by appropriate learning and experience. I discussed in Chapter 1 how physical traits are affected by certain environments and experiences. Somehow, when behavior is involved, many people forget that almost any characteristic can be changed and assume that if intelligence is mostly inherited, it cannot be improved by experience. The truth is that traits regarded as inherited may simply require new and better programs of stimulation and education than we now possess.

Evidence for a genetic contribution to intelligence does not necessarily mean that differences between races or ethnic groups are also associated with genetic differences. Many groups of people who immigrated to the United States at first tended to score poorly on standardized IQ tests, and this fact was sometimes attributed to poorer genes for intelligence. Some decades later, however, these same groups had improved their scores relative to the remainder of the American population. Presumably, early cultural differences caused the initially poor performance. American Jews are a prime example: originally they scored more poorly than non-Jews, but now they are substantially overrepresented in the highest levels of mental-test performance.

How, then, shall we think of intelligence? Being intelligent is a little like being an athlete. Athletics encompass many diverse skills, including distance running, weight lifting, rowing, archery, ping-pong, and so forth. While there is a tendency for individuals who are agile, strong, and fast afoot to be good at a variety of athletic events, they do not excel at all of them. A weight lifter is not likely to be a good high jumper, an American football lineman may be quite clumsy at soccer, and sprinters may be terrible at gymnastics. Moreover, though all of us would agree that certain natural physical abilities are necessary for certain sports (say, running speed for track, football, basketball), each characteristic must be nurtured and then mixed with other skills that are primarily acquired through training (strength, endurance, positioning, strategy). Without the opportunity to develop these additional skills, the person's natural potential will not be achieved. Finally, societies value different athletic skills—the definition of a "good athlete" varies from country to country. European soccer stars are relatively unknown in the United States and American baseball and football heroes are not recognized in Europe. So, too, "intelligence" has many facets, some of which are valued more highly by one culture than another. While people are undoubtedly born with different potential abilities, opportunity and experience are required for any skill to flower, and that joint developmental process starts in infancy.

Intelligent behavior in a four-month-old infant is simply not the same thing as intelligent behavior in a two-year-old. The two-year-old can talk, for example. Moreover, studies show that infants of a given age who are advanced at one "mental" skill are not necessarily advanced at another, and children who score well on infant tests of mental development at six months do not necessarily do well at twelve or twenty-four months. Parents whose children do not walk or speak as early as others should take heart: these facts alone usually do not predict later intellectual behavior.

The role of stimulation. We have all heard that infants need to be "stimulated" and that the proper intellectual environment must be provided for children before they reach school age lest they be permanently disadvantaged. Is this true?

Infants and children should be gently stimulated and encouraged, and some activities are likely to be more beneficial than others. Most parents who care about their infants play with them and give them periods of undivided attention every day. These interactions will probably include simple games of "you-talk-and-then-I'll talk" or peek-a-boo, naming objects, and exploring. Beginning at approximately eighteen months and continuing throughout childhood and adolescence, a good environment probably includes caregivers who rely on language and are fluent in its use; exposure to a variety of objects, events, and information; activities that exercise a child's memory, imagination, and thought; adults who match their informal teaching to a child's current abilities and interests; and learning experiences that the child enjoys.

Even if a child does not have these experiences, it is possible for him or her to be a "late bloomer," one who is not intellectually skilled early in life but becomes so as an adolescent or an adult. And, as we have seen, there are a few cases of children who were grossly neglected or deprived during early childhood who nevertheless managed to achieve essentially average intellectual performance after a few years of more normal experience. Therefore, some psychologists believe that a child's intellectual potential is not locked into place at age three or six. Most children and even adults are at least potentially capable of becoming more intelligent—"brighter" if you will.

A commonplace illustration of this development can be seen by attending one's ten- or twenty-year high school reunion. Most of the good students have achieved some success in life. But, in addition, a few of those people who barely made it through high school found their niche later and are now in positions of responsibility, influence, and wealth. This seems to be particularly true of men, perhaps because society demanded that they, more than women, "make something of themselves."

Good environments must change with a child's growing abilities. One cannot simply give a child the "best" intellectual environment between six and twelve months and expect that shot of nurturance to be sufficient for the rest of the child's life. Mental development is dynamic and continues to change its character across the years of childhood, and there is no experiential inoculation at any age that will guarantee mental competence later. Therefore, parents are advised to have a good time with their infants, be sensitive to their changing needs, and play games and provide experiences that seem to match their child's abilities and interests at the moment.

Early Learning

Infants certainly learn, and in some circumstances they can learn quite well. But the requirements for infant learning are more stringent than for adults.

TYPES OF LEARNING

One of the earliest forms of learning consists of recognizing that an object or event is familiar. If an event occurs repeatedly, an infant may respond to it the first few times it happens but not thereafter. In a sense, they recognize the event, become bored with it, and stop responding.

Dr. Steven Friedman demonstrated that infants in the first few days of life can learn and remember a simple visual pattern. Friedman presented newborns with a black and white checkerboard. He showed it repeatedly for one-minute periods until the newborns' attention to it began to fall off sharply. Presumably the infants had become familiar with the checkerboard. To ascertain that the infants had not just become drowsy without learning anything about the checkerboard, Friedman changed the pattern slightly by increasing or decreasing the number of checks in the design. The babies immediately perked up and studied the changed stimulus with renewed attention. Moreover, the greater the difference between the new and the old checkerboards, the more the infants looked. This resurgence of interest indicated that the infants had indeed "learned" the first stimulus and detected that the checkerboard had changed.

Parents can demonstrate a similar kind of rudimentary learning even with infants a few weeks old. Take a penlight flashlight and shine it into the eyes of a drowsy or quietly alert infant. If the light is rather bright, the infant may wince or tighten the eyes, only to relax when the light is withdrawn. If the light is again focused on the eye after a few seconds, then removed, and repeated, the infant may eventually make no response at all, presumably a sign of familiarity with this periodically appearing light.

In fact, such learning is possible even before birth. Dr. Lester Sontag at the Fels Research Institute in Yellow Springs, Ohio, repeatedly made a loud noise near the abdomen of pregnant women while monitoring the heartbeat of the fetus. At first, the heart rate increased, demonstrating that the fetus had heard the sound and responded to it. After many repetitions of the sound, however, the fetus made no response unless a different noise was sounded.

Infants are also able to learn from experience when certain events are likely to occur. In one study, a group of infants was placed on a three-hour feeding schedule from birth while another group was fed every four hours. After a few days, the three-hour infants became restless and ready to eat if food was not provided in three hours, whereas the four-hour infants did not become agitated until after four hours. Apparently each group had learned when its feedings were supposed to take place.

Infants in the first few months of life are also capable of more intricate learning. While at the University of Rochester, Dr. Arnold Sameroff investigated whether infants could learn to change their sucking behavior if it meant more milk for them. As described in Chapter 3, sucking consists of at least two processes, negative pressure and biting. Sameroff engineered a special nipple that allowed him to detect when babies sucked with negative pressure and when they sucked by biting. Milk could be delivered almost immediately when one or the other of these behaviors occurred. Infants in the first few days of life were quite capable of learning to bite and not to produce negative pressure if milk was delivered only for biting; other babies learned to create more negative pressure and less biting if milk was delivered only for negative pressure. After they had learned which behavior was being rewarded, Sameroff changed the rules, and infants who had been rewarded for biting were now rewarded for negative pressure, and the reverse. The babies quickly learned to change to the other sucking strategy to keep the milk coming.

Infants can also learn the subtle rules that govern the behavior of their mothers during feeding. Dr. Kenneth Kaye at the University of Chicago observed that mothers typically hold their infants still when they are sucking. But when infants pause in their sucking, some mothers will talk and jiggle their infants, as if to encourage sucking and feeding. Sometimes infants enjoy this social game and will actually increase the frequency and length of their pauses between bouts of sucking, thereby obtaining more talking and jiggling. They have learned to do something that influences their mothers.

GUIDELINES TO INFANT LEARNING

There are certain requirements for early learning. First, what infants learn is usually related to something they already know or do quite well. It is no accident that they learn about looking, sucking, and physical contact most easily—these behaviors are already well practiced and important to their survival.

Second, if infants are going to change their behavior, something must happen to encourage that change. In the case of Sameroff's experiment, milk was given for one but not another behavior, and the infant was thereby encouraged to bite or to produce negative pressure. According to Kaye's observations, talking and jiggling by the mother apparently encouraged infants to stop sucking, and the baby's pauses encouraged their mothers to jiggle them.

A third requirement is that such encouragement or "reward" must be delivered immediately following the infant's response. Dr. Stuart Millar in Scotland showed that unless the encouragement follows the infant's actions by only a second or two, infants do not associate the encouragement with their behavior. They don't understand that they are supposed to repeat what they just did to get more encouragement.

Fourth, the encouragement must be clearly associated with the behavior to be learned. The vocalizations of a two-month-old baby can be increased by an adult who smiles at and responds to every sound. But if the adult smiles and talks to the baby continually, regardless of whether the infant is babbling or not, the infant is not likely to understand that the adult's actions are meant specifically to encourage vocalization.

Finally, infants are individuals. They have different likes and dislikes, moods, and skills. Some infants may learn to coo if a parent jiggles them after each vocalization; others will learn to smile but not coo; still others will prefer a "surprise face" to jiggling. Again, the best clue to how well the adult's activity is matched to the infant is whether the infant is having a good time playing.

These requirements for learning are fairly restrictive. In fact, Dr. John Watson of the University of California at Berkeley feels that while infants in the first few months of life are capable of learning a variety of things, they actually learn very little because these circumstances are not often met in the home—parents either do not respond to the infant's actions or they respond too slowly or too inconsistently.

Parents may be able to see their three- to five-month-old infant learn at home by following the above guidelines. For example, infants can be placed in a crib with a brightly colored piece of yarn loosely tied at one end to the infant's wrist and to a mobile or balloon at the other end. Infants may soon learn that the mobile will move when they wave their arm. Moreover, they may learn to wiggle only the arm that is attached to the yarn, thus showing that they "know" which arm produces the spectacle. If the infant doesn't learn, it means nothing and should be forgotten. Learning games of this sort are more fun if the infant's response produces smiling or talking from another person, not a jiggle in a mobile.

Stages of Mental Growth

Mental ability consists of more than learning one movement or another. For one thing, there must be an understanding of the nature of the world, and for the infant this knowledge seems to develop in stages. Moreover, intelligence is not something that remains basically the same and simply grows larger in some sense from age to age. Intelligence goes through a series of major qualitatively different steps characterized by the presence of some and the absence of other abilities.

Although its nature changes, intelligence seems to serve at least two common functions throughout life. First, newborns, toddlers, children, and adults are highly disposed to acquiring information about the environment—objects, people, themselves. The ability of the individual to understand information changes greatly with development, but the function of acquiring information remains the same. Newborns focus their eyes on the corners or light-dark edges of a visual form—the point of the greatest visual information. Adults read books, attend lectures, and tinker with clocks and radios. These behaviors are very different, but each brings information to the individual. Without this tendency and a memory able to store and retrieve such knowledge, humans (and other organisms) would not profit from experience, adapt to changing environments, or even survive.

The second function of intelligence is to influence or control the environment, both objects and people. Adaptation depends not only on learning what the environment looks and sounds like, but also on the individual's ability to control it and make it work. Toddlers manipulate, throw, and tear up toys and other things; children try to influence and control their parents, teachers, and other children; adults seed clouds to make it rain, convince others to buy a given product, and build space capsules out of metals, liquids, and gases in the environment. Humans are environment tamers and controllers.

If we keep these two notions in mind—acquiring information and influencing the environment—many of the profound changes in behavior from infancy to adulthood can be understood, not as a sequence of isolated skills but as different stitches in a single piece of cloth.

THE FIRST TWO MONTHS

By adult standards, intelligence in the first few months of life is hardly intelligent at all. For the most part, it consists of exercising the sensory, perceptual, and physical abilities with which infants are born. Infants look, listen, touch, grasp, suck, and taste; this seems to be a time to exercise these basic functions. In fact, infants and toddlers frequently rehearse newly acquired skills over and over again—it is a common theme in development.

Acquiring knowledge. Infants tend to look at objects that are distinctive—sharp visual edges of high contrast, corners, or movement. They are not merely sponges of anything that comes into view, but selective about what attracts and holds their attention.

As we have seen, even very young infants can learn and remember—they can recognize the smell of their mother's breast, the sound of her voice, and even her visual appearance. But, when an infant "recognizes" the mother, it is probably not as complete or rich an experience as it is later. Infants in the first few weeks of life tend to concentrate their attention on the perimeter of a face—the hairline and chin. Therefore, when infants in the first weeks of life visually "recognize" their parent, they probably do so primarily on the basis of facial outline, hairline, or color rather than the eyes, nose, and mouth on which adults rely. By two months of age, infants focus on the eyes and other interior features of the face. Not only do two-month-old babies look at their parent's eyes—perhaps because of their high brightness contrast—but they will smile at a face only if the eyes are open. At present, scientists cannot say whether these tendencies are inborn, learned because parents encourage eye-to-eye contact, or both.

Infants can also imitate actions they see other people do, if those actions are ones the infant already practices. Drs. Andrew Meltzoff and M. Keith Moore of the University of Washington found that infants in the first few weeks of life imitate adults who stick out their tongue and move their fingers at the babies. Actually, this is a remarkable feat. How do infants translate the visual perception of someone else's movements into their own actions, especially mouth movements? Infants cannot see themselves move their mouths or tongues. How do they know they are doing exactly what the adult did without watching themselves? Apparently infants are born with some kind of ability that permits them to imitate certain actions they see others do even if they cannot watch themselves perform that action.

But imitation in the first few months of life is very selective. First, infants do not imitate each and every action they see. To be imitated, a behavior must be something that the infant already does frequently. For example, infants are more likely to imitate adults sticking out their tongues than adults who say "bah-bah-bah." Infants in the first months of life frequently stick out their tongues of their own accord. But, while they can utter the syllable *bah*, they do not often do so spontaneously.

Second, infants will imitate only in special circumstances. Adults must be close enough for the infant to see their behavior clearly; the adults' behavior must be highly distinctive (for instance, the only movement of

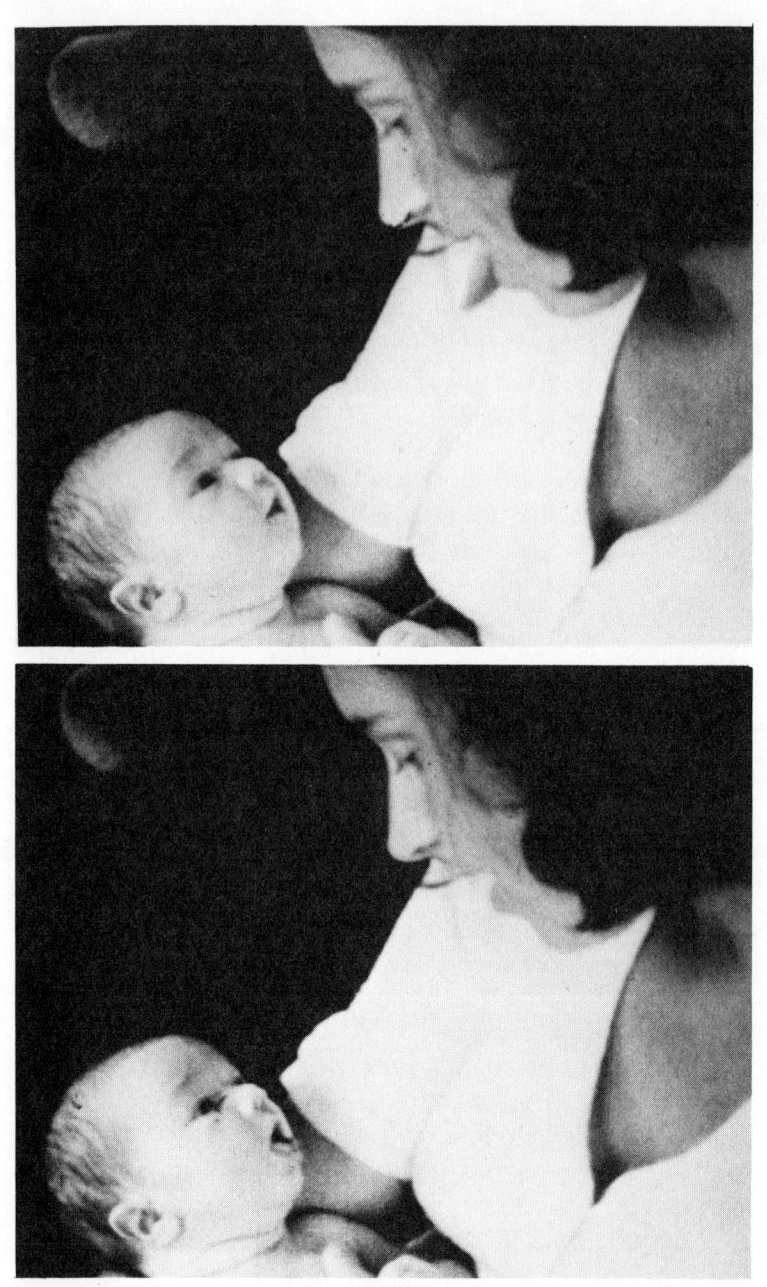

This six-day-old baby has never seen himself stick out his tongue, but somehow he "imitates" his mother's action.

the face should be made by the tongue); and adults must wait patiently for the baby to perform. After sticking out their tongues, adults should wait motionless, sometimes as long as fifteen or twenty seconds, before trying it again because the sight of their moving face will distract the infant from imitating.

The world is me. Although young infants are capable of perceiving a good part of the environment, learning actions, and remembering events, the infant's understanding of the world is quite subjective. Young infants do not know that the environment is separate from themselves or from their actions with it. Objects and people are known by what infants do with them, including looking, listening, and touching. To the infant, "the world is what I do with it." A bottle is something to suck and a mother is something to look at or touch. Moreover, when an object or a parent is out of the infant's sight, it is literally out of mind. Infants cry when their mother leaves; but once she is gone, she temporarily does not exist for the infant. "The world is me and what I do."

Two to Seven Months

Acquiring knowledge. By two months of age, the infant can see the world much better than at birth, and vision is essentially 20/20 by six months of age. But 20/20 vision does not necessarily mean that the infant understands the world in the same way adults do. Up until now, babies have perceived the world as a collection of unrelated stimuli. Infants have been able to remember specific features of an object and detect when such features change, but they have not paid attention to how the specific elements of an object are arranged with respect to one another—to a very young infant a face may have been a collage of hair, eyes, nose, and mouth. At approximately three to five months of age, infants begin to organize and integrate these features into a pattern that is more similar to what adults know as a face.

The infant's memory during this stage can be quite good. Dr. Joseph Fagan at Case Western Reserve University has shown that six-month-old babies who are given only a minute or so to look at a simple geometric pattern can remember it one or two weeks later. Infants were allowed to "study" a pattern on one day, and then several days later they were shown that familiar picture plus a new picture. Even after a week or two, infants spent more time looking at the new pattern, regardless of what it actually was, presumably because they remembered the familiar picture and "knew that already." Therefore, four- to seven-month-old infants probably know and remember their parents whose faces are now seen as integrated wholes rather than as collections of familiar features. The information that the infant is acquiring is becoming more complex and organized.

Influencing. One of the greatest advancements in this period is the emerging ability of the infant to reach for, grasp, and manipulate objects. This provides the infant with a chance to influence the environment. Many objects make noise, change shape, or otherwise "respond" to manipulation. They permit the infant not only to answer the question "What is this?" but also "What can I *do* with this?" Responsive toys are ideal for this purpose because they tend to react without delay every time the infant squeezes, shakes, or throws them. People, not just toys, can and should provide the infant with similar experiences. There is no reason why adults cannot widen their eyes and say "beep" every time an infant squeezes their nose. If they respond quickly, consistently, and distinctively, even very young infants will explore this opportunity to influence and control them. Besides, these silly games are fun—for both parent and infant.

Reaching and grasping. The opportunity to secure objects for exploration and influencing depends upon the infant's ability to reach for and grasp objects, a skill that goes through some remarkable transitions in the course of its development. Dr. Jerome Bruner and his colleagues at Oxford University have studied in great detail the infant's emerging ability to secure an attractive object. During the first few months of life, infants have a grasping reflex similar to that of birds, monkeys, and other animals. A small oblong object, such as a finger or the stem of a rattle, placed in the infant's palm will elicit a rather strong grasp. More often than not, the baby is likely to bring hand to mouth and suck on the object.

Bruner believes that the hand-to-mouth sequence is an inborn behavioral pattern. Sometimes, a two- to five-month-old infant who is grasping an object will actually begin mouth movements before the object arrives there. Bruner claims that if one sticks a finger in such an infant's mouth before the object arrives, this event completes the sequence and the baby will drop the object before actually sucking it.

But the grasp-and-suck sequence is only one aspect of reaching for objects. At first, two- to three-month infants will only grasp objects presented directly in front of them. If an object is held out to one side, infants are likely to turn their head and shoulders toward the object and not reach out until the object is directly in front of them. Even then, both hands may shoot out for the rattle or ball. Soon, however, infants will reach for toys presented to one side or the other without turning their bodies, and in a unique way. It is as if the infant is straddling a glass wall that reaches from the nose outward and separates the space in front into right and left "rooms." Objects on the right are reached by the right hand, and objects on the left side are grasped with the left hand. Sometimes this tendency is so strong that if the infant is having trouble grabbing hold of an object

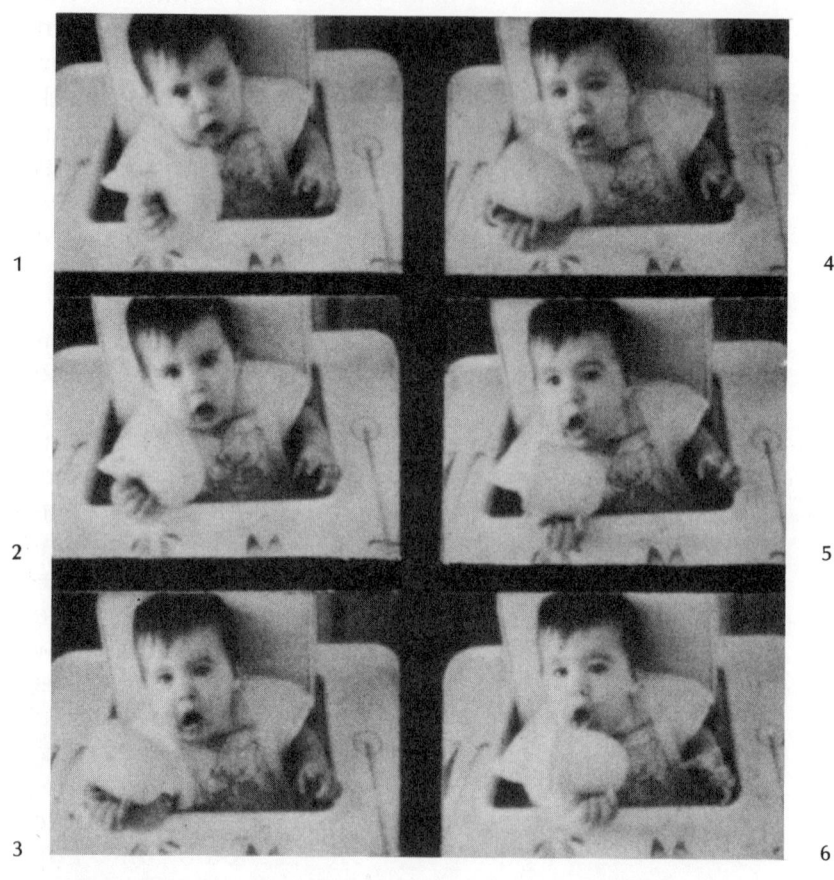

A child illustrates the hand-to-mouth sequence. The cup is on his right side, so he reaches with only his right arm. Once he has grasped the cup, he opens his mouth in anticipation of receiving it.

on the right side, the left hand dangles helplessly and does not come to the aid of the right until the object moves toward the middle of the body and is finally seized by both hands. Eventually, around five months of age, the imaginary glass wall disappears and objects on either side will be grasped with either hand.

During the course of this development, the infant is amazingly accurate at finding an object with the hand. Bruner has shown that once an object is sighted by the infant, the eyes may close while the hand shoots out after it, usually making a direct hit without the aid of vision. Even if a large bib is tied around the infant's neck and stretched out in front at shoulder height while an attractive object is held out at the end of the bib, infants seem to be able to reach for the object quite accurately. Apparently infants do not need to see their arms or hands to direct their reaching.

Out of sight and mind. Although the infant's sensory and physical skills have improved greatly, the child's understanding of the world is still severely limited. The environment remains very personal for the infant. Objects still do not exist apart from the infant's actions or perceptions of them. They grasp and manipulate one object in essentially the same way as another—they do not tailor their actions to fit the specific character of the object; they do not explore the diverse attributes of a toy, and they do not imitate new behaviors (although they may perform familiar actions more frequently if an adult also performs them).

All of this derives from the fact that infants behave as if objects do not have an independence of their own. A rattle is a "thing of my hand" or a "noise when I shake my arm." It is not an oblong toy with a bulb containing beads that can produce a sound if manipulated in the proper manner.

The world is still so tied to the infant's own perceptions and actions that people and objects literally do not

A six-month-old infant has no sense of object permanency, so when a toy elephant is blocked from her view, she doesn't seem to understand that it is still in place. On the other hand, an older child can transcend the towel barrier to find a hidden toy.

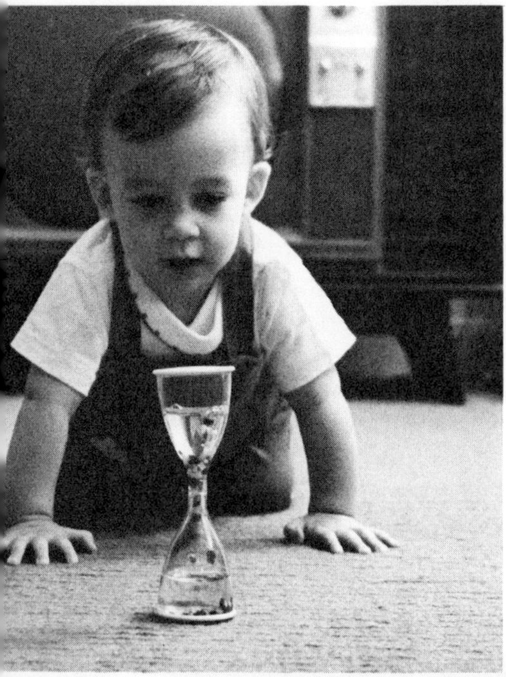

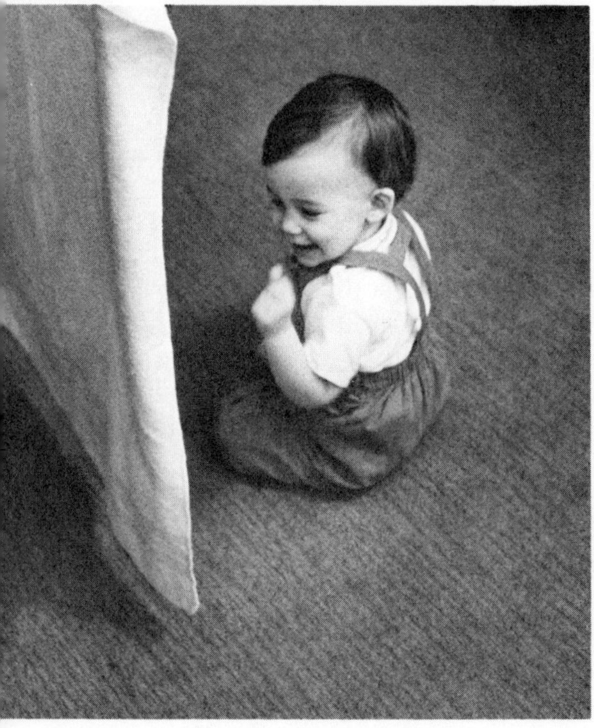

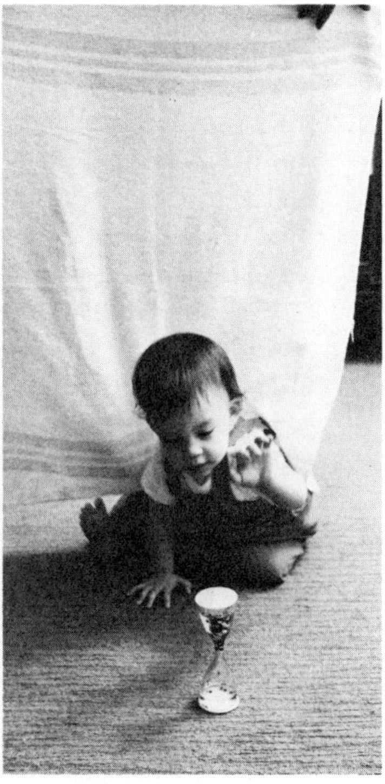

exist when they cannot be seen, heard, or touched directly. Jean Piaget, the renowned Swiss scholar, performed a little experiment with his own children. He showed a toy to each of his children when they were five or six months of age. With the infant watching, he hid the toy under a coverlet so that only a portion of the object could be seen. The child reached for and retrieved the object. This was repeated three times. The next time, however, again with each infant watching intently, Piaget hid the toy totally out of sight. Even though the infants saw their father hide the object, they behaved as if the object had disappeared and crawled away to other entertainment. Out of sight is out of mind.

SEVEN TO THIRTEEN MONTHS

The world is not me. Sometime between six and eight months of age, infants make an important advancement. They begin to understand that toys that were once "objects of my hand" are now "objects out there to be grasped." This change may not sound momentous, but it is. First of all, objects and people now exist for the infant even when they are not present. Piaget discovered that at this age infants would find the toy even when totally hidden.

Some parents notice their infant's ability to understand the permanence of objects in another way. Their infant plays "dropsy" by frequently dropping objects off the tray of a highchair. Prior to six or eight months, the spoon that falls overboard may make an interesting noise, but the infant does not look over the side of the tray to search for it. Once it is out of sight and has stopped clanging on the floor, it is gone. Now, however, the spoon continues to "exist" on the floor even when it isn't making a noise, and some infants will nearly fall out of their highchair looking for it. Moreover, if an attentive caregiver is willing to pick up the spoon and replace it on the tray, the infant is just as willing to throw it down, again and again. It's a wonderful game—at least for the infant, who is relishing the exercise of a newfound skill and enjoying some influence over another person.

Influencing. A second consequence of attaining this stage is that objects now possess characteristics to be explored, and the features of one toy may require a different method of exploration than the features of another. In short, infants begin to match their exploratory manipulation to fit the specific characteristics of objects.

Moreover, infants begin to take a more intense interest in how they can affect objects. Piaget noticed that babies at this age love to play with toys that produce sounds or move in unpredictable ways. One such toy is a ball that rolls in irregular paths and makes chimelike sounds as it weaves about the floor. At first, infants may freeze in rapt attention as the ball rocks back and forth playing its tune. Then, suddenly, they will seize the ball and let it roll out of their grasp in essentially the same way they did the first time, again watching the consequences. It is the sequence of action, pause and look, repeat action, pause and look, that signifies an infant's interest in the characteristics of objects "out there."

Memory. Another mental advance of this period is that the child can remember something about objects and events when they are not present. Not only do absent objects exist, but they are located in a certain place, have a specific color, and move in a specific way. Up to this point, infants remember toys, people, and cause-effect sequences, but they do so only if they are reminded of them. Infants will remember that the chime ball makes a noise and rolls in a funny way, but only when they see it in front of them. Now the ball exists even when it is absent.

One attribute of an object that can be remembered is its name. Of course, eight-month-old infants usually cannot say any words, even "mama" or "dada" let alone "ball" or "doggie." But they can understand in a limited way the name of an object when an adult says it. Parents often play games with their eight- to ten-month-old infants that rely on this ability. They might hold up a red ball and, when the infant studies it intently, say *"Ball, this is a ball."* With repetitions of this tutoring, the child will come to associate the word *ball* with that object, even though the child cannot pronounce the word. Now comes the crucial part of the game. If the child is allowed to play with the ball and leaves it out of sight in a corner, the parent may ask the child *"Where is your ball?"* Children of this age are sometimes (but not always) able to find the ball if they are asked soon after they leave the toy, thus demonstrating that they remember something about the object (its name and location) even when they can't see it.

Stimulation and toys. Parents often want to know what they can do to help their child develop. Obviously infants need people and objects to look at, listen to, and touch. They seem most fascinated by things that respond in some way when handled. Mobiles, chime balls, a long flexible coiled spring, crumply paper, pots and pans, and all manner of other objects that can be made to do something are ideal toys (assuming, of course, they have no sharp edges, cannot be easily broken, and may be put into the mouth with some safety). But social games are really best. The parent who quickly responds in an exaggerated way to an infant's actions is also a great "toy." Parents can teach their nine- to twelve-month-old infants the names of certain objects (especially in one-syllable labels) and can exercise the child's use of names and memory by asking the infant to find the toy without pointing or otherwise indicating where it is. Regardless of the game, the most important rule is for parent and child to enjoy it.

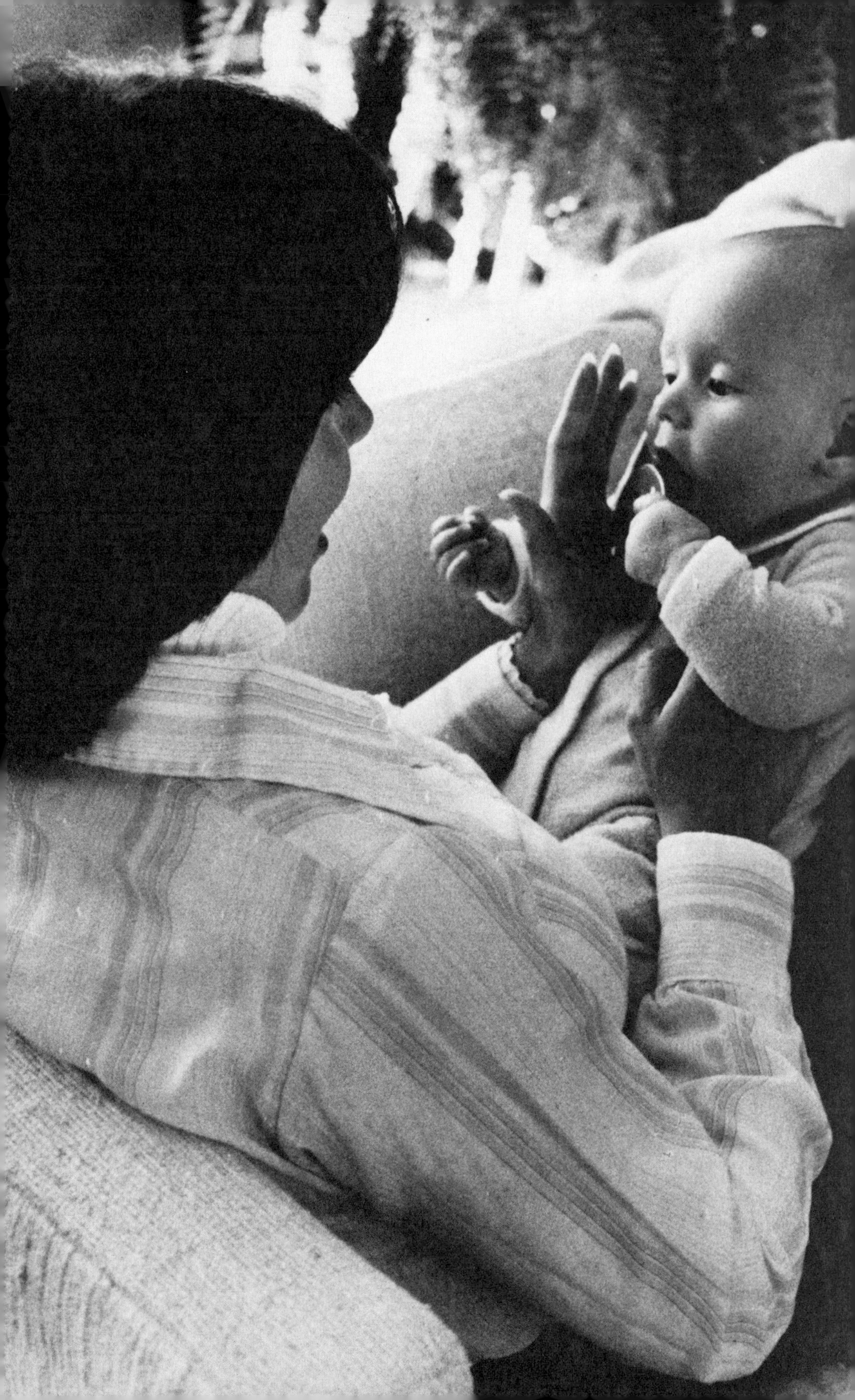

Chapter Six
Personality and the Growth of Attachment

JOHN B. WATSON, an American psychologist influential in the early 1900s, believed that the early experiences of children determined their capabilities and personalities. He accepted John Locke's concept of a *tabula rasa:* infants were born as blank slates upon which the fingers of experience would inscribe the dimensions of their personalities. Watson boasted that if any infant were placed in his charge, he could steer its development in any direction he chose, creating rich man, statesman, beggar, or thief. As we have seen, psychologists still believe in the vital role of experience, but not to the exclusion of other factors. Infants are born with certain temperamental differences that blend with the personal style of their parents and with specific life experiences.

Probably the first personal and social task for infant and parents is to develop affection for one another. The growth of love derives from a meshing of infant and parent behaviors—doing things together. It is fostered on the one hand by certain characteristics of the infant and, on the other, by the parents' ability to adapt, to be appropriately responsive to the infant's behavior, and to respect and encourage the infant's active role in the process.

Early Dispositions

During the first month or two, infants concentrate on adapting their bodies to life outside the womb. As we have seen, they do not come into the world without preparation. Infants are born with different temperamental characteristics, although these personal styles will undergo profound transformations in the course of development. Nearly every mother of two or more children has sensed the differences between her infants even before they were born.

Temperaments

Infants seem to be born with their own personalities. Drs. Alexander Thomas, Stella Chess, and Herbert Birch in New York studied the personality growth of 141 children from 85 families from birth through ten years of age. While this group was somewhat special (well-educated and containing a large number of Jewish families), the results of the study nevertheless help us to understand different kinds of temperament and personal types from infancy through childhood.

Thomas, Chess, and Birch describe nine different temperamental characteristics of the children as determined by interviews with their parents. The major categories include:

Activity. Some infants seem to be very vigorous and physically active. They constantly squirm and kick, and as toddlers they may shake and throw toys with gusto. Other children are more placid, moving slowly and less intensively. This is one of the first temperamental characteristics sensed by mothers. Even before birth, some fetuses move and kick more than others, and at least one study shows that fetal activity may be related to behavioral differences in children as late as two years of age.

Not every active fetus or infant remains active, but

some do. Thomas, Chess, and Birch describe one such case:

> Donald exhibited an extremely high activity level almost from birth. At three months, his parents reported, he wiggled and moved about a great deal while asleep in his crib. At six months he "swam like a fish" while being bathed. At 12 months he still squirmed constantly while he was being dressed or washed. At 15 months he was "very fast and busy"; his parents found themselves "always chasing after him." At two years he was "constantly in motion, jumping and climbing." At three he would "climb like a monkey and run like an unleashed puppy." In kindergarten his teacher reported humorously that he would "hang from the walls and climb on the ceiling." By the time he was seven Donald was encountering difficulty in school because he was unable to sit still long enough to learn anything and disturbed the other children by moving rapidly about the classroom. (A. Thomas, S. Chess, and H. G. Birch, "The Origin of Personality," *Scientific American*, 1970, 223, 104.)

Parents should not assume that because their child kicks a lot in the womb or splashes vigorously in the tub at six months that school problems are inevitable seven or eight years later. There is considerably more change than stability in personality from infancy to childhood.

Irritability. All infants cry, but in varying degrees. Some babies become easily distressed at the introduction of any new food, person, or event. They cannot stand change in their daily routine. At an older age, trivial circumstances may trigger unrestrained screeching and tantrums. Other infants seem to control their crying, stop easily on their own, and readily adapt to changes in their environment.

Social responsivity. Some infants love to be held, kissed, and rolled about in their parents' arms. They are "cuddlers." Later they may smile and babble a lot and are easily engaged in talk and play. As children or adults we would call them gregarious or extroverted. Other infants may stiffen and resist being held. They appear serious and do not smile or babble very much. As children they are considered introverts, preferring to play alone.

Personality Styles

A personality has many dimensions. Infants are combinations of these and several other temperamental dispositions. Thomas, Chess, and Birch found approximately 65 percent of the children they studied to be of three types: easy, difficult, or slow-to-warm-up.

Easy children. By far, most children were regarded as easy. These researchers described them as having

> positiveness in mood, regularity in bodily functions, a low or moderate intensity of reaction, adaptability and a positive approach to, rather than withdrawal from, new situations. In infancy these children quickly establish regular sleeping and feeding schedules, are generally cheerful and adapt quickly to new routines, new foods and new people. As they grow older they learn the rules of new games quickly, participate readily in new activities and adapt easily to school.

Difficult children. A much smaller group was considered difficult.

> These children are irregular in bodily functions, are usually intense in their reactions, tend to withdraw in the face of new stimuli, are slow to adapt to changes in the environment and are generally negative in mood. As infants they are often irregular in feeding and sleeping, are slow to accept new foods, take a long time to adjust to new routines or activities and tend to cry a great deal. Their crying and their laughter are characteristically loud. Frustration usually

sends them into a violent tantrum. These children are, of course, a trial to their parents and require a high degree of consistency and tolerance in their upbringing.

One characteristic of this group is the high intensity with which such children respond to certain situations. Clem was such a child.

> At four and a half months he screamed every time he was bathed, according to his parents' report. His reactions were "not discriminating—all or none." At six months during feeding he screamed "at the sight of the spoon approaching his mouth." At nine and a half months he was generally "either in a very good mood, laughing or chuckling," or else screaming. "He laughed so hard playing peekaboo he got hiccups." At two years his parents reported: "He screams bloody murder when he's being dressed." At seven they related: "When he's frustrated, as for example when he doesn't hit a ball very far, he stomps around, his voice goes up to its highest level, his eyes get red and occasionally fill with tears. Once he went up to his room when this occurred and screamed for half an hour."

Slow-to-warm-up children. Thomas, Chess, and Birch described a third group of a few children who "typically have a low activity level, tend to withdraw on their first exposure to new stimuli, are slow to adapt, are somewhat negative in mood and respond to situations with a low intensity of reaction."

Every child is different and no child remains entirely the same from infancy to adulthood. Even those children classified as one of these three types did not possess all of the traits listed as typical of that type. Moreover, one out of every three children could not be classified into these three groups, and even those who were so designated at one age did not necessarily retain the characteristics of that designation at a later age. Indeed, one study has shown that 60 percent to 70 percent of the four-to-eight-month infants wind up in totally different temperamental categories by three to seven years of age. These descriptions provide a useful way to think about early personality, and they emphasize that some children are born with pronounced temperaments of one sort or another. But parents should not jump to the conclusion that a fussy eater, for example, will be "difficult" in every respect now and forever more.

The really important lesson is that parents cannot treat each infant or child the same way and expect the same result, even within the same family. Suppose both husband and wife have careers, are busy people and are slightly quick-tempered. This is their natural style. If this couple has an easy child, things may work out rather well for both infant and parents. But what if their infant happens to be difficult? Such children require considerable tolerance and patience. Life for all members of this family could be one emotional, screaming battle after another.

On the other hand, thoroughly doting parents, who may be ideally suited for coping with a difficult infant, might have problems with the slow-to-warm-up child. When such an infant refuses to eat new foods or shies away from new toys, people, or experiences, the parents might not push the issue. That approach might work, but in the extreme the child could also become isolated from the world, never learn to deal with new situations, continue to be shy, and fail to cope with peers. Thus, while acceptance might work for the difficult infant, some gentle encouragement might be necessary with a timid child.

The main point is that the roots of development, especially personality, social behavior, and attachment, do not reside in either infant or parent alone. Rather, development depends on how parents and infants relate to one another, on the sensitivity of parents to adapt their behavior to the specific needs of the child, and on the responsiveness of parents and infants to the social overtures of one another.

Socializing in the First Six Months

Several things must happen before attachment develops between infant and parents. The infant must be able to sense the parent and to remember which people are familiar and which are not. But simply perceiving and remembering a parent are not sufficient. As adults, we remember quite well many individuals for whom we have little personal affinity. Something else is required. Somehow parent and infant must be able to communicate with and influence each other.

THE INFANT'S COMMUNICATION

Infants are able to communicate with their caregivers only in limited ways, but they can be effective.

Looking. I have already said that the most important method of infant communication is eye-to-eye contact. It is just about the only way the infant can be a full partner in social relations, since the infant can initiate, maintain, and terminate a social exchange with a caregiver by looking into his or her eyes, by continuing to look, and by turning the eyes away.

Crying. Crying is the baby's way of calling for attention. Of course a parent must heed this request and keep the infant safe and comfortable; but responding to the infant's cry is also important for social reasons. Studies have shown that when infants are calmed after a crying episode, they are often ready to look, listen, and play with their parent.

Babies cry for a variety of reasons. As we have seen, some infants cry more than others. In one study, some infants were found to cry as much as eight times more than others during a twenty-four-hour period. Other studies have shown that infants of mothers who received substantial anesthetic during delivery tend to cry more later than infants whose mothers did not have anesthetic; mothers who are anxious or under stress tend to have infants who cry more; infants born after long labors cry more than infants born quickly; boys tend to cry more than girls and circumcised males more than uncircumcised; and certain cultural groups (say, American) cry more than others (say, Chinese). Although there is a slight tendency, especially among boys, for infants who cry a good deal to be somewhat more tense later in childhood, for the most part crying in infancy is governed by specific, temporary circumstances, and it does not predict how irritable the infant will be later.

Some of these temporary circumstances are quite common. Babies cry when they are hungry. Mothers who breast-feed are sometimes touchy about this fact. Indeed, the biggest single reason mothers stop breast feeding is that they think their infant cries excessively and that this stems from an inability to produce enough milk. Actually, research shows that in many cases the infants of breast-feeding mothers cry just as much as those who are bottle-fed.

Infants will also cry if they are too cold or too hot. It may be that cold infants sleep less deeply and are therefore more easily aroused by noises and events around them.

Sometimes a wet diaper will lead to crying, although the fussiness may be associated more with the loss of temperature accompanying evaporation than with the wetness per se.

Infants also cry, of course, when they are in pain. An accidental prick from an open pin will generate a justified screech. An intestinal upset, especially colic, can produce unusual crying, most often in the evening, although the reasons for the upset are less clear. More than half of the babies studied by Drs. Martin Richards and Judy Dunn at Cambridge University cried regularly in the evenings at two months of age, and breast-fed infants cried somewhat more than bottle-fed babies. In another survey, Dr. Ronald Illingworth of Children's Hospital and the University of Sheffield, England, found that approximately 21 percent of otherwise healthy babies suffered from colic. Many theories concerning the cause of extreme irritability in young infants have been offered, but Illingworth could find no evidence that overfeeding, underfeeding, allergy, constipation, diarrhea, gas, or too much or too little handling caused the condition. Many parents feel that regular evening crying is a sign of a spoiled child, but the amount of attention parents pay to a child seems unrelated to colic—in Illingworth's study, 33 out of 49 cases of colic began in the hospital before the baby went home.

What will stop crying? Obviously the first thing is to alleviate the circumstance producing the crying. Some people believe that even newborn babies give their parents a clue to the problem by crying differently when they are hungry than when they are in pain. Some adults also think infants have a special cry to indicate when they are angry. Moreover, nurses who care for infants in the hospital can often identify infants from their cries alone, and mothers quickly become able to distinguish the cry of their own baby from that of another. In fact, not only do mothers recognize their own infant, but their bodies respond to that perception by a rushing of blood and milk to the surface of the breast in preparation for feeding.

No matter whether infants actually have a "cry vocabulary," even the most conscientious parents often cannot determine the cause of their infant's distress. After a thorough check for pins, wetness, hunger, and temperature, the infant still wails. What can a parent do then?

Holding and rocking an infant has a calming effect. In studies at Stanford University by Drs. Anneliese Korner, Rose Grobstein, and Evelyn Thoman, crying babies who were picked up and put on the shoulder were more likely not only to stop crying but also to open their eyes and look about more than infants who were either merely propped up to a sitting position or infants who were left alone in their cribs. Moreover, it was the experience of being moved about while being picked up that was responsible for soothing the infants and encouraging visual alertness.

And psychologists have even gone so far as to prove that there is an "optimum rock." Dr. Anthony Ambrose in London and Dr. Lewis Lipsitt at Brown University used a special rocking machine to determine that such movement does indeed calm infants. With the infants they studied, 60 rocks a minute with a draw of 7 cm (2¾ inches) seemed to work best.

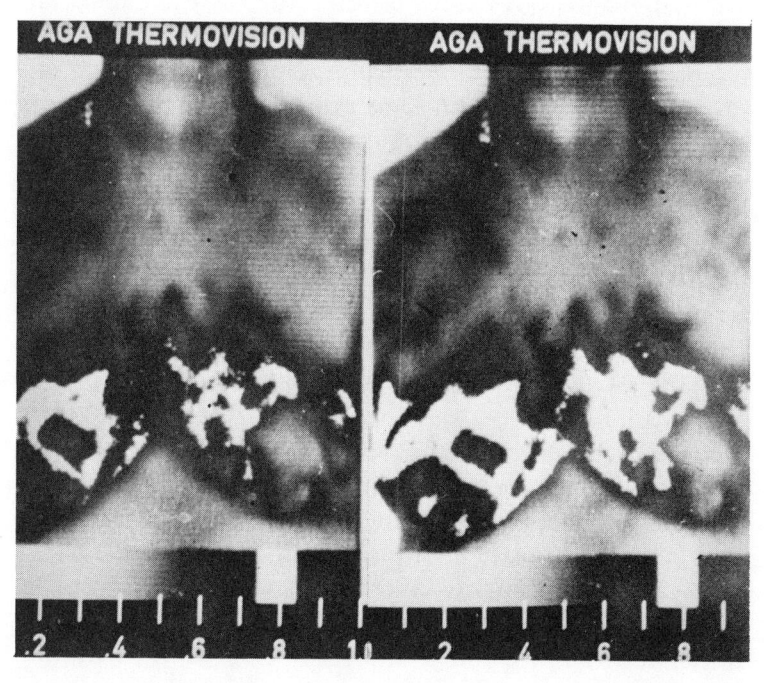

A crying infant elicits a physical response in the mother. In these thermographs of a mother's breasts, the dark areas are cool spots and the light areas hot. The heat increases markedly from one picture to the next as the mother responds to her baby's cries.

Moving or rocking quiets infants, but allowing them to move uncontrollably on their own does not. One of the oldest known methods of calming an infant is swaddling, wrapping the infant securely in a blanket and thereby restricting arms and legs. Recently scientists have attempted to determine what it is about swaddling that works so well. Drs. Peter Wolff at Children's Medical Center in Boston and Yvonne Brackbill at the University of Florida have attempted to determine whether it is the temperature, skin contact, or restraint of movement associated with swaddling that produces the calming. Wolff found that babies who were naked but kept quite warm cried more than swaddled infants, an observation that apparently eliminates temperature as the causal factor. Brackbill's research points to the restraint of movement more than the close-fitting wrap as the crucial factor. Why does it work? One guess is that often young infants get wound up and can't seem to control their gyrating arms and legs. Swaddling may help them inhibit these movements and stop crying.

Sucking also has a calming effect. Sucking steadies the heart rate, relaxes the movements of the stomach, and inhibits thrashing of the arms and legs. But if an infant is crying because of hunger, eating is much more effective. Of course, parents quickly find that sucking has a calming effect, and this is often the beginning of the use of pacifiers.

It also helps to have something for the infant to listen to or look at. Some authorities have suggested playing recorded heartbeat sounds in the newborn nursery as a way to calm infants, and it does seem to work. Originally this was explained by suggesting that the fetus had associated hearing the mother's heartbeat with the serenity and security of the womb. Some have even claimed that this intrauterine sound experience is the basis of later proclivities to rhythm and dance. These are intriguing thoughts, but they are probably not true. Studies by Brackbill have demonstrated that nearly any constant or rhythmic stimulation has the same effect. Also, a recording of a person's heartbeat taken through a stethoscope is not at all like heartbeats sound to the fetus. There is a great deal of noise in the womb—the thump of the mother's heartbeat is mixed with the rushing pulse of blood, and the sound increases as the fetus grows and stretches the abdominal blood vessels.

What is interesting about this science of calming a crying baby is that mothers apparently have "known" how to do it for generations. If an infant is crying, an experienced mother or grandmother is likely to pick up the infant, envelop it in her arms, rock it gently, lean over and place her face directly in front of the baby, and talk or sing. In short, she incorporates almost everything science has discovered about calming an infant into one choreographed set of actions. Not only does this quiet the baby, but it sets the stage for mutual eye contact and play.

Smiling. Nothing entrances parents more than their infant's smile. However, the very young infant is probably not directing the smile at them. In fact, even blind babies smile during the first months of life, and normal babies tend to smile most when they are not very attentive to the parent, such as during states of irregular sleep and drowsiness.

But, by the second and third months of life, the infant begins to smile at certain stimuli. The research of Rolf Ahrens has shown that infants of this age smile mostly in response to the eyes. However, it is not "eyes" per se, because according to one study young infants will smile even more if there are several black dots on a piece of white paper. With development, the infant will no longer smile at dots—something more human is necessary. By the fourth month, when smiling reaches a peak, a complete outline of the face is required, and infants begin to smile mostly at their familiar caregivers, although some will also smile at complete strangers. Smiling also occurs in nonsocial contexts. For example, an infant who struggles successfully to understand or remember a given stimulus may celebrate that conquest with a smile.

Research by Dr. Martin Richards at Cambridge University demonstrated that the smile can be generated by social interaction with the parent, but only according to certain rules. An infant may watch a parent smile. Then, the baby gradually becomes more and more active, eventually reaching a crescendo, at which point the infant pauses to study the parent again and then releases a burst of energy in a smile. Usually parents cease all movement as the baby builds up excitement, as if in anticipation of the smile. If parents do not wait patiently during this period but talk or otherwise stimulate the infant, the smile may be lost and the infant can become

Over the period of the first few months of life, different levels of facial features and expressions are required to elicit the infant's smile.

upset and even cry. This is a perfect example of how a parent's behavior must be phased with the infant's, and how mutual satisfaction derives from the sensitivity of each partner to the behavior of the other.

COMMUNICATION

Communicating with an infant requires the parent to adopt some special strategies. In fact, parents behave quite differently with an infant than they do with another adult, and these special communication behaviors accommodate to the infant's more limited capabilities and dispositions.

Special faces. Dr. Daniel Stern of the Cornell University Medical Center is a keen observer of the fine detail of social play between mothers and their infants. In addition to using a high-pitched, singsong voice and short, repetitive sentences, adults make special faces for infants. Stern describes several, all characterized by exaggerated and slow facial movements. One is the mock-surprise expression, in which the adult's eyes open very wide, the eyebrows rise, the mouth opens, and the head tilts up slightly. This movement pattern is often accompanied by an "oooooh" or "aaaaah." Although there are many variations from adult to adult and situation to situation, the basic elements are the same—slow motion and an overly animated expression of surprise.

A second expression is the frown, consisting of knitting the eyebrows and narrowing the eyes, tilting the head to the side and downward, pursing the mouth, and wrinkling the nose. The accompanying sound is something like "aaaaooooh," with a progressive drop in pitch and volume toward the end. Other expressions include smiles, displays of concern, and a blank face.

These faces seem to communicate something to young infants. For example the mock-surprise expression serves to invite the infant to join in social play. It is a greeting, and it frequently does get the infant's attention. The smile and an expression of concern serve to maintain the interaction and provide feedback to the infant about how it is going. The frown ends an interaction; and an expressionless face, particularly if the parent then looks away, signals to the infant that the caregiver is not ready or interested in playing.

In all of these expressions, the exaggeration helps the infant to attend to them and to learn what they mean. The accompanying vocalizations are higher in pitch and volume and punctuated with greater variations in sound levels than is usually the case. Moreover, the pauses between parental utterances are longer, as if to permit the infant time to understand and respond.

Looking. Even the way parents look at infants is substantially different from the way they look at adults. In adult social relations two people typically do not look into each other's eyes without talking for more than about ten seconds, but Stern found that mothers and infants often remain locked in mutual gaze for thirty or more seconds, sometimes in utter silence. Moreover, in adult conversation the listener looks at the speaker most of the time, but the speaker looks at the listener primarily at the beginning and the end of the monologue. In contrast, mothers were found to gaze at and vocalize to their infant simultaneously. Moreover, they spent nearly 70 percent of playtime looking at their infant, with an average duration of approximately twenty seconds, which is quite long by adult standards. However, when feeding the infant, mothers do not look and vocalize simultaneously, perhaps because this combination is too strong an invitation for the infant to play and would thus interrupt the feeding.

RESPONSIVE PLAY

We have seen that early attachment between parent and child requires that the infant be able to perceive, remember, and communicate with the parent. But at least one more factor is needed—infant and parent must relate to one another in more elaborate ways than the simple signaling of cries and smiles. Many psychologists believe that attachment will not blossom without something we might call "contingent responsiveness": when the infant performs a certain action, the parent responds immediately in a distinctive way that is matched to the infant's behavior. If the baby burps, a parent may quickly respond with a mock-surprise expression which, by its nature, means something special to the infant. The baby may smile in return, and so the social exchange continues.

When one thinks about it, contingent responsiveness is the definition of social behavior—people responding to one another appropriately and reciprocally. If an adult says something, the listener usually verbally responds to it; if one person gives another a teasing pat on the back, the second may respond by feigning a counterattack. The important features are that one person's response occurs immediately after another's; one behavior is related in some particular way to the preceding action; and both partners understand and enjoy the exchange.

Contingent responsiveness is such an obvious component of adult social behavior that it seems pedantic to mention it. The notion is more subtle but no less crucial to parent-infant relationships and the growth of love and attachment. Adults respond to each other with the same type of behaviors (as in talking) and typically understand the actions of the other. But, infants have only a few social responses they can make (looking, crying, smiling) and they are incapable of all but the most rudimentary understanding of their parents' actions. A vast psychological gap appears to separate parents from infants. The wondrous thing, as we have already seen, is that nature seems to have planned several bridges over this chasm.

The sensitive parent. Dr. Mary Ainsworth at the University of Virginia has studied parent-infant relationships for many years. She describes a sensitive mother—one who generously provides contingent responsiveness to her infant—in the following way:

> The sensitive mother is able to see things from her baby's point of view. She is tuned-in to receive her baby's signals: she interprets them correctly, and she responds to them promptly and appropriately. Although she nearly always gives the baby what he seems to want, when she does not she is tactful in acknowledging his communication and in offering an acceptable alternative. She makes her responses temporally contingent upon the baby's signals and communications. The sensitive mother, by definition, cannot be rejecting, interfering, or ignoring.
>
> The insensitive mother, on the other hand, gears her interventions and initiations of interactions almost exclusively in terms of her own wishes, moods, and activities. She tends either to distort the implications of her baby's communications, interpreting them in the light of her own wishes or defenses, or not to respond to them at all. (M. D. S. Ainsworth, S. M. Bell, and D. J. Stayton, "Individual Differences in Strange-Situation Behavior of One-Year-Olds." In H. R. Schaffer, ed., *The Origins of Human Social Relations* [London and New York: Academic Press, 1971, pp. 17–52].)

Sensitive parents can have an influence on their infant as early as the first weeks of life. Dr. Lewis Sander at the Boston University School of Medicine observed the consequences of different styles of parenting. Infants were retained in the newborn nursery for the first ten days of their lives and then transferred to a special ward where they were cared for by either one of two nurses who differed in their caregiving styles. One nurse responded quickly and efficiently to the cries of her infants, but in a slightly stereotypic manner. The other nurse, who was described as more sensitive and adaptable to the individual differences of her infants, was more likely to modify her behavior to fit the specific infant and situation.

Sander reported two major results. First, infants cried more during the first ten days in the hospital nursery than later when the two nurses could respond more readily to their calls for attention. Second, the infants tended by the nurse who was less adaptable to individual differences cried more than those assigned to the more sensitive nurse.

A quick, consistent, and relevant response is the hallmark of a sensitive parent. This was demonstrated by Dr. John Watson at the University of California at Berkeley. Watson put a special pillow under the heads of two-month-old infants. When the babies moved their heads, the pillow relayed that information to a mobile hanging above the crib; the mobile immediately turned around for a few seconds, thereby jiggling the several hanging parts. The babies were delighted and were soon shaking their heads to move the mobile and smiling and cooing. Their mothers reported that they had hardly smiled before this time and that they had never been so excited and happy.

One father tried a similar game with his eight-week-old daughter. The infant sat on the father's knee while he held her hands and arms securely in his hands. Then, with a relatively expressionless face, he waited and waited and waited, until the little girl eventually sighed. Instantly, he bounced her gently on his knee, gave a broad smile, and said, "Bumpty-bump." Then his face went blank, and he waited again, until his daughter produced another vocalization to which he responded in precisely the same way. On the first day the game lasted for ten minutes, and the baby sighed and gurgled only three times. The next day, the pace quickened, and by the third day the eight-weeker was a veritable chatterbox. But the most important thing was that father and daughter literally fell in love with one another. In fact, when the father came home from work after a week of such games, all he had to do was lean over the crib and his little girl would coo and smile at him. It made the mother rather mad, because she was spending her entire days caring for the infant but the father was getting all the smiles.

There are many lessons in this example. First, the father responded immediately to one particular behavior of the child—vocalizing. A swift response was necessary for the child to associate the father's behavior with her own vocalization. Next, the father made himself and his response as distinctive as possible. The blank face helped make the "bumpty-bumps" stand out; they were not lost in a stream of conversation and other facial expressions. And bouncing, smiling, and talking are behaviors babies "understand." Moreover, the father responded consistently, every time the infant vocalized. Finally, less than ten minutes a day for a few days was all that was required for that father and infant to become attached to one another.

Deviations from Nature's Plan

For the most part, nature has disposed adults toward appropriate and sensitive responding to infants. When the responses of caregiver and infant are harmoniously meshed, affection is the product; when infant and caregiver are out of tune with each other, frustration and unhappiness may be the result. What would happen if infants had no responsive caregiver?

Fortunately, there are not many children in the world who have suffered such a deprivation. However, a few studies report dismal conditions in certain orphanages in which infants receive only minimal care and few social experiences with adults. Observers have described such children as being without emotion or energy, helpless, and depressed, some were even thought to die as a result, though that is difficult to prove. Children reared for the first three years of life in such institutions have been found to differ from those reared in foster homes in three major ways: institution-reared children are more aggressive and antisocial, more dependent on adults, and more distractable and hyperactive.

Learned helplessness. One of the most pronounced characteristics of these institutionalized children is their apparent helplessness. Some psychologists have emphasized that when a caregiver responds appropriately to an infant, the infant learns that it has some influence: "I can do things that have an effect on objects and other people." Later that child says, "I can do things that help myself." On the other hand, children who are not exposed to toys and sensitive adults may learn the opposite: "I can do nothing to influence the world" and later, "I can do nothing to help myself achieve the things I want." In short, they may learn to be helpless: "Why should I try to do anything. Nothing does any good."

Studies with animals confirm that this is possible. Some years ago, Dr. Richard Solomon and his colleagues at the University of Pennsylvania placed some dogs on one side of a rectangular box with a barrier in the middle. A few seconds after a sound, the dogs were subjected to a strong electric shock and prevented by the barrier from escaping to the other side of the box. Later the partition was removed, and the dogs were tested to see if they would now escape the shock by jumping over the hurdle to the safe side. Even after experiencing only a few of the inescapable shocks, the dogs learned that they could do nothing and so failed to flee the shock even after the partition was removed. More recent research with other animals by Dr. Martin Seligman at the University of Pennsylvania indicates animals that have learned to be helpless in one situation are often helpless in other contexts.

Can this happen to humans? Many developmental psychologists think it can. In the course of his studies of infants and mobiles, Watson found that infants whose parents purchased a commercially available wind-up mobile that twirls independently of the infant's behavior did not learn to make Watson's mobile twirl. In fact, they were less capable at this task than infants who had no particular experience with mobiles. Watson is careful to point out that at this stage one does not know if infants experienced with wind-up mobiles are also less capable of learning different tasks than this one. Nevertheless, this observation does illustrate that, in at least one specific situation, human infants apparently can learn not to respond—that is, to be "helpless."

Studies of older children who do not achieve in school suggest that a major contributor may be this same attitude of helplessness. Children who succeed on school tests frequently indicate that they "studied hard" or that they "are good in math." In contrast, children who do poorly often blame circumstances other than themselves—"those are the breaks of the game" or they were "just unlucky."

Short separations. Children are occasionally separated from their parents, as when they must be isolated for a week or more in a hospital. Studies show that such a separation can have a distressing effect on the infant, and many hospitals have taken steps to minimize this consequence.

Dr. Michael Rutter of University Hospital in London has reviewed the scientific studies on the effects of separation. He concludes that a few nights apart does not create obvious intellectual or emotional deficits, but longer separation can produce increased antisocial behavior, at least for a time, especially when the separation is caused by family discord.

Dr. James Douglas of the London School of Economics studied the behavior of adolescents born in Great Britain who had been admitted to a hospital for more than a week or hospitalized repeatedly when under the age of five. As adolescents, these children worked less hard in school, encountered more reading problems, were more troublesome and delinquent outside of school, and showed more unstable job patterns.

When infants or young children are separated from their parents for reasons of prolonged hospitalization or transference to public care, they react with clear distress. Dr. Rudolph Schaffer of the University of Strathclyde in Scotland has studied many such cases. Citing John Bowlby, he describes these children as going through three phases of response:

> first a period of distress, when the child cries for his mother and refuses to be looked after by anyone else; then a period of despair, during which he becomes quiet and apathetic; and finally a period of detachment, when he appears to come to terms with the situation but at the cost of his emotional tie with his mother and his ability to put his trust into any relationship. There can be a number of variations on this theme—if, for example, a substitute mother is available he may become attached to her in the third phase. Nevertheless, children between approximately six months and five years of age are most likely to react in this way to separation. In addition, when the separation is temporary, the child is further unsettled for a period when he returns home: he may initially continue to be detached and treat his parents like strangers, though subsequently he will go to the opposite extreme and become over dependent and clinging, refusing ever to be left alone. (*Mothering* [Cambridge: Harvard University Press, 1977], pp. 96–97.)

Enlightened hospital policy is to have parents spend as much time with their children while they are in the hospital and to have auxiliary staff available to play with the infants and meet their emotional as well as medical needs.

Mismatches between parents and their infants. Parents and infants do not need to be separated for the attachment process to go awry. Infants, even those within the same family, have different temperaments and personalities. So do their parents: one parental style may be ideally suited for one infant temperament but quite disturbing for another. What happens when there is a mismatch? The result may be frustration, unhappiness, and failure to develop a mutually satisfying and affectionate relationship. Infants and parents are often more adaptable than we suppose, and things frequently work out in the long run. But sometimes, they don't.

Daniel Stern discusses several types of mismatches. One, of course, is the unresponsive parent who provides caretaking services but little in the way of contingent, reciprocal, sensitive, and playful socializing. Unhappily, many fathers fall into this category. The result may be an infant who displays relatively less life, less emotion, less excitement. It is a mild case of "helplessness."

Another common pattern is the intrusive parent, who is constantly stimulating and playing with the infant but does not allow the infant a chance to contribute to the interaction. Stern calls this the chase-and-dodge pattern in which the parent constantly pursues the infant who tries to escape, unsuccessfully. Stern vividly describes one case of a mother who wanted continual, exciting, animated interaction and her three-month-old daughter, who wanted to have a chance to lead too.

> Whenever a moment of mutual gaze occurred, the mother went immediately into high-gear stimulating behaviors, producing a profusion of fully displayed, high-intensity, facial and vocal infant-elicited social behavior. Jenny invariably broke gaze rapidly. Her mother never interpreted this temporary face and gaze aversion as a cue to lower her level of behavior, nor would she let Jenny self-control the level by gaining distance. Instead, she would swing her head around following Jenny's to reestablish the full-face position. Once the mother achieved this, she would reinitiate the same level of stimulation with a new arrangement of facial and vocal combinations. Jenny again turned away, pushing her face further into the pillow to try to break all visual contact. Again, instead of holding back, the mother continued to chase Jenny . . . She also escalated the level of her stimulation even more by adding touching and tick-

ling to the unabated flow of vocal and facial behaviors . . . With Jenny's head now pinned in the corner, the baby's next recourse was to perform a "pass-through." She rapidly swung her face from one side to the other right past her mother's face. When her face crossed the mother's face, in the face-to-face zone, Jenny closed her eyes to avoid any mutual visual contact and only reopened them after the head aversion was established on the other side. (*The First Relationship* [Cambridge: Harvard University Press, 1977], pp. 110–111.)

The sequence continued, the mother pursuing contact and the child avoiding it, until both were quite upset. In this particular case, the story ended happily—the mother eventually learned to hold back and let Jenny control the situation for a few moments.

Sometimes the chase-and-dodge game is played with more playfulness, and therefore is less oppressive to the infant. The mother will pause after the child looks away, as if to give the infant time to regroup, then, when the infant looks back at her, she resumes the chase but at a lower level of excitement and intensity.

Six to Twelve Months—Specific Attachments

Between approximately six and eight months of age, some dramatic changes take place in the social behavior of infants. As we saw in Chapter 5, infants now begin to distinguish between their actions and the consequences of those actions. Further, at this stage, more clearly than before, the infant displays attachments to particular individuals—typically the parents.

STRANGERS AND SEPARATION

Up to this point, while infants smiled more at their parents, some would also smile at strangers. Further, whereas infants might become upset when a parent left, they would protest being left alone by anyone and would greet a stranger almost as happily as their own parent.

Now things are radically different. For some infants, changes begin to occur at five or six months. Strangers are viewed warily. A stranger, especially one who rapidly approaches the infant, may produce a sober, staring, apprehensive expression on the infant's face. By seven to nine months, the rapid approach of a stranger, especially one who reaches out to touch the infant, may produce crying. Similarly, infants of this age vehemently protest being left alone by their parents.

Why do infants become upset at separation from their parents or at the approach of a stranger? Why doesn't this happen before six to eight months of age? Psychologists are not quite sure why these phenomena occur, but they have several ideas.

First, infants of this age now understand that their parents exist even when they are out of sight. This advancement permits the child to understand that the absent parent is available for summoning. Second, the infant's memory is better. It is possible to remember people, objects, and events, even when they are absent. Although these two factors are necessary, they are not sufficient to explain why the child becomes upset in such situations. Many researchers have speculated that infants imagined what might happen in the absence of their parents or what a stranger might do to threaten or harm them. Other scientists do not believe that infants are capable of such symbolic reasoning and imagination until quite some time later.

An alternative guess involves the infant's uncertainty over what to do in this situation. Prior to this age, infants did not understand that people were independent of the infant's own actions: people were the direct and indistinguishable consequences of the infant's looking, listening, and behaving. Now, however, the infant suddenly understands that people are capable of doing things on their own. The task for the infant is now "What can I do to keep my parent here?" and "What will I have to do in the presence of this stranger?" Therefore, according to this view, infants become upset because of uncertainty over what to do, rather than fear.

This guess is supported by several observations. First, when a stranger enters the room and stands some distance away, infants may attend to the stranger with some wariness but usually they do not cry until the stranger approaches quickly or reaches out to touch them. In contrast, if the stranger talks with the infant's mother, smiles and converses with the infant, and approaches quite slowly, infants are far less likely to become distressed. Presumably, rapid approach and touching demand a response from the infant, and a casual approach by the stranger allows the infant time to adjust. Moreover, if the stranger plays games familiar to the infant, infants are not as fearful. Perhaps the game represents "something to do," thus eliminating the infant's uncertainty about what response to make. It seems that when the infant is suddenly called upon to make a response and doesn't know what to do, distress results.

If you think about it, adults become upset under the same circumstances. Just for the sake of argument, suppose a Martian appeared and quickly approached. As long as the Martian stayed well enough away, we would be apprehensive but not devastated. But let the Martian come at us in a hurry, and we would be terrified—not only because we would imagine what might *happen to us* (and adults are old enough to imagine such things), but because we would be frantic over what we *should do* to deal with the situation.

If this analysis is correct, what should parents do? First, they need to understand that this is typical, normal infant behavior that occurs between approximately seven and twenty-one months of age. Second, parents can warn adults who come to the house that they should talk together for a while before attention is paid to the infant. Third, let the child come to the stranger. Fourth, parents might try teaching their infant to do something in situations of approach and departure: to say "bye-bye" and wave at them when they depart and to say "hi" and shake hands when they return. If this is a common, well-learned pattern of behavior, the infant will have something to do that is familiar when being left alone as well as something to do when strange people arrive.

One mother always told her older toddler to "have a good time" whenever he went to his playroom or left on an outing with his father or grandparents. This child rarely became upset at being left with a babysitter, and when older he would stand at the door and tell his departing parents to have a good time. Teaching a child a response to make at separation or when a stranger approaches may not eliminate the problem, but it might help.

Part Four
The Second Year

Chapter Seven
First Words

DURING THEIR FIRST YEAR, infants live in their own world; during the second year, they live in ours. They explore every corner and thing in the house. They talk and demand to be heard. They have a mind of their own and defiantly say no to their parents' requests. The toddler aspires to all the rights and privileges of the human fraternity. The second year can be an exasperating experience for parents, but it is also a period of profound accomplishment.

Two major triumphs of the mind mark the second year of life. The first, occurring at approximately thirteen months, is the infant's newfound ability to make mental connections between two objects in the environment without having to act on those objects directly. The second, beginning at approximately twenty-one months, is the ability to use symbols to think about objects that are not actually present. These basic mental advances permit the emergence of the most remarkable of human abilities—language.

The child's understanding of the relationship between self and the environment is a basic theme in early mental development. As we have seen, during the first year of life, infants progress from knowing the world only through their own actions to an understanding that objects and people are somehow separate and different from them. However, even though the child is beginning to understand the difference between actions and the objects acted upon, the two realms are not totally distinct until early in the second year.

Relations between Objects

Around thirteen months, toddlers begin to comprehend not only that their actions are distinguishable from the objects in the environment but also that the two can be totally independent. The child now has a clear understanding that parents perform actions on their own quite apart from the infant's actions, vocalizing, or other behavior. Moreover, some toys possess certain dynamic properties: the car goes by itself; the doll talks of its own accord. And toys may be found in several places, not just where the infant last left them.

THE OBJECTIVE WORLD

Parents can see this development emerge with the simple hiding game described earlier. If you take a small object like a toy duck and hide it under a blanket or a pillow, a seven-month-old will find it only if some part is left sticking out in view. A ten-month-old child will not have the same difficulty, but will be baffled by a new kind of disappearing trick. Let the infant find the duck under a blanket several times. Then in full view, hide the duck under a different cover. The ten-monther will still look for it in its first hiding place. At approximately thirteen months the child solves this puzzle too. The transition is a sign that the infant has advanced beyond knowing the world only through actions on it ("the object exists where I found it the last time"). Now objects exist when they are out of sight and their locations are not dependent on the infant's actions. However, suppose the object is completely hidden from view under one cover and the infant finds it there several times. In full view of the infant, the object is now placed under the first cover and then withdrawn; placed under a second and then withdrawn; and placed under a third and left there completely hidden. During the early part of the second year, toddlers will become quite adept at looking for the object where it last disappeared. But now suppose that the adult tricks the infant and, instead of leaving the toy under the third cover, conceals it in hand. Infants between twelve and eighteen months are befuddled—they will not infer that the toy must be in the adult's hand or some other place. In short, they have achieved some cleverness and flexibility in relating objects to one another (toy with covers), but they cannot symbolically imagine what might happen to an object when it is out of sight. Their thought is still tied to the world they see and hear; they can only escape the here-and-now when they can think with symbols—at approximately twenty-one months.

Another capability that emerges at around thirteen months is the toddler's ability to understand relationships between two objects in the environment without having to act on them. Prior to this stage, an infant playing with a tea set might have knocked any two objects together to produce an enjoyable sound. A cup and the table, a spoon and the teapot, a saucer and the child's head—any pair would have done. In each case, the infant discovered a relationship between the action (shaking or hitting two objects together) and the sound—the nature of the objects was more or less irrelevant. Now, however, the infant realizes that cups belong on saucers, teapots are tipped toward teacups, and spoons are stirred in cups. Having seen these objects used together by other people, the infant is able to associate cup with saucer, pot with cup, and spoon with cup without having actually handled these objects before.

Now two things, neither one of which is tied to the infant's actions, are related to one another in the infant's mind. This is a monumental advance, because infants now understand that there is an unexplored world out there, separate from them or their actions, composed of objects and people, many of which cannot be touched but which nevertheless relate in many ways to other objects and people. Objects have names; puzzle pieces go together in certain ways; and small pans fit into big pans that belong in kitchen cabinets.

IMITATION

Much of this new world can be discovered simply by watching others. Toddlers are now capable of imitating a variety of common social behaviors that they see adults perform: objects that are miniature replicas of common household implements (dustpan and broom, dishes, hammer, saw) make interesting toys at this age. Toddlers can imitate sequences of actions. Whereas younger infants could repeat a single action, now they can link two separate actions together in a meaningful sequence. Suppose a parent cracks an egg into a bowl and then beats it with a whisk. The infant might imitate smashing the egg, but would forget what to do next. Not so the toddler, who is capable of putting both actions together in a coordinated sequence.

But there is a curious limitation to the toddler's ability to imitate, the same limitation that prevents a child of this age from finding the toy that the adult surreptitiously fails to hide under one of the three covers. That is, the child cannot symbolically represent objects that are not present.

This is a subtle distinction, but it is vitally important from the standpoint of the child's mental development. Children between thirteen and twenty-one months will pretend to pour tea from a pot to a cup and will drink from that cup, but they will not offer a cup of tea to a doll. One explanation is that they do not really imagine the presence of tea—they are merely imitating pouring actions and drinking actions (pots are lifted and pointed at cups; cups are raised to the lips). It is only after about twenty-one months that they can imagine tea and mentally pretend to help a doll drink it. Notice that helping a doll drink tea is an action they never see other persons do; they cannot do such things until later in the second year.

Play

Finally, play with toys and objects becomes much more systematic. Toddlers are able to experiment a little by varying actions with objects to observe the diverse consequences. The infant in the first year will repeatedly shake a "slinky," a long coiled spring, and observe its writhing, snakelike movement. But the infant will shake it in essentially the same way each time. In contrast, the toddler will thrash it from side to side, then up and down, again in a circular pattern, and finally throw it across the room, presumably for the purpose of watching the different outcomes produced by these diverse acts. This is an experiment, done more to find out what the *object* can be made to do than what the *infant* can do.

Words

The ability to relate one thing in the environment to another without physically acting on either object permits the child to learn language. Words are sound patterns that become associated with specific objects. Of course, infants often learn to say "mama" or "dada" before their first birthdays, and they can learn that a plastic dog has a certain name and shape associated with it. But some psychologists feel that these feats are not true vocabulary. They represent simple associative learning, similar to learning their name or that a father's putting on a coat means he will leave soon. The child does not understand that the label can be *separated* from the specific object and applied to other objects. True vocabulary requires that the label and the object be understood as associated but potentially separate things. The toddler of eleven to fourteen months is mentally able to do this.

Symbolic Relations

Between eighteen and twenty-four months the child develops the ability to symbolize objects and events that are not present. It is the dawn of true thought. When the adult conceals the toy while pretending to place it beneath one of the covers and actually hides the object behind the back, toddlers of this age are likely to figure out that the object must still be in the adult's hand.

Moreover, two-year-olds can imagine tea in a teapot or in a cup that they offer to a doll. And toddlers can combine two unrelated objects to accomplish a specific purpose. They will bring a chair to the kitchen counter to reach the cookie jar. The child exhibits symbolic thought, evidenced in part because the child has never before seen another person perform these acts and is still able to put the elements of the behavior together.

The same symbolism permits the transportation of memories and images of actions through time and space. Two-year-olds who see their mothers or fathers working in the kitchen or the shop may remember what their parents did in that context and imitate a whole sequence of actions several days later, in another place and with pretend objects.

Language. The ability to symbolize objects and relationships between objects grants the child the ability to put words together to form new thoughts. Up to this point, toddlers may understand the words "dog" or "ball" as well as "run" or "allgone." When they see a dog running across the yard, they may point and say "dog" or "run." Now they can combine those two words to say "dog run," and in the next breath recombine these and other words to describe a whole host of events—"dog allgone," "dog bye-bye."

The emergence of the ability to symbolize allows toddlers to do things that involve mental rather than action experimentation and to recombine objects and actions into new relationships, perhaps ones that do not really exist in the world. In many respects, this advance represents the emergence of true thinking, even imagination.

The philosopher Jacob Bronowski poetically expressed this wondrous accomplishment and its special contribution to the human species in *The Ascent of Man*. After discussing some of the earliest human art—the manufacture of tools and the drawing of animals and hunts on cave walls—Bronowski observed: "The men who made the weapons and the men who made the paintings were . . . anticipating a future as only men can do, inferring what is to come from what is here. There are many gifts that are unique in man; but at the center of them all, the root from which all knowledge flows, lies the ability to draw conclusions from what we see to what we do not see, to move our minds through space and time, and to recognize ourselves in the past on the steps to the present." And the most magnificent vehicle of this symbolic thought, which sets humanity apart from most other species, is the extent and variety of our language.

The Roots of Language

A child's first word is a momentous occasion. The variety of language is one of man's unique capabilities, and in the eyes of parents the toddler's first utterance seems to transform the infant into a new species. Language is a marvelous achievement, but it is even more fascinating to see the order and logic in its development.

Anyone who has studied a second language, especially its grammar, discovers how really complex it is. Nevertheless, most children acquire the basic rules of grammar by about the age of six, despite the fact that

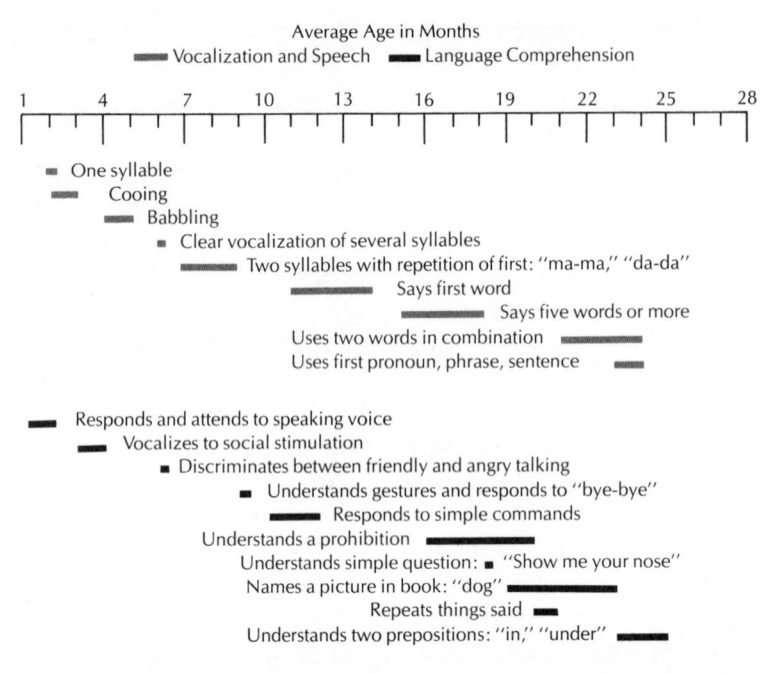

```
                    Average Age in Months
         ━━ Vocalization and Speech   ━━ Language Comprehension
 1      4      7      10     13     16     19     22     25     28
 ├──┬──┬──┬──┬──┬──┬──┬──┬──┬──┬──┬──┬──┬──┬──┬──┬──┬──┤
        ■ One syllable
          ━━ Cooing
              ━━ Babbling
                  ■ Clear vocalization of several syllables
                     ━━━━ Two syllables with repetition of first: "ma-ma," "da-da"
                              ━━━━ Says first word
                                       ━━━━━ Says five words or more
                            Uses two words in combination ━━━━
                            Uses first pronoun, phrase, sentence  ━
 ━━ Responds and attends to speaking voice
     ━━ Vocalizes to social stimulation
          ■ Discriminates between friendly and angry talking
              ■ Understands gestures and responds to "bye-bye"
                  ━━━ Responds to simple commands
      Understands a prohibition ━━━━
           Understands simple question: ■  "Show me your nose"
           Names a picture in book: "dog" ━━━━
                     Repeats things said ━
           Understands two prepositions: "in," "under" ━━━
```

Some of the language milestones that occur in the first two years of life. The average ages indicated are approximations, and the lengths of the lines show the range of ages resulting from a compilation of several studies.

most parents do not teach them directly, cannot state the rules of grammar if asked, and typically do not speak to their child in complete, well-formed sentences.

Roadblocks. In fact, one wonders how children ever learn proper language, given what they usually hear in everyday conversation. When two people talk to one another, their grammar is often atrocious. Sentences run on interminably, phrases are linked into long strings or imbedded one within another, and the subject is frequently unspoken. Moreover, when adults speak to children, they often use baby talk and imitate the incorrect phrases they hear their children speak. Yet even children of immigrant parents who do not speak the local language well eventually learn not only the grammar but correct pronunciation. And children of deaf parents who hear normally also seem to progress quite well.

Speed of learning. Despite the monumental task and what seems to be miserable circumstances for learning, children acquire language at an incredible pace. Most children begin to babble at about six months, utter their first word at approximately one year (although quite normal children may not accomplish this until after eighteen months of age), begin to combine words into two-word sentences by two years, and have essentially mastered most aspects of their speaking grammar by five to six years of age.

The blistering speed of language acquisition can be seen clearly in the growth of vocabulary. By one estimate, the average one-year-old knows about three words, but this increases to approximately 22 words by eighteen months, 272 by twenty-four months, 896 by three years, and 1540 by four years. The typical three-year-old is acquiring approximately two new words a day!

Language is the ability to put words into combinations to express new thoughts. Consequently, when children get to the two-word stage, new combinations literally cascade from their lips. One language specialist attempted to count the number of different two-word combinations his two-year-old child produced every month. His month-to-month estimates were 14, 24, 54, 89, 350, 1400, and 2500. Near the end of this string, the child was creating four new two-word combinations every waking hour.

The ability to form new combinations with such rapidity gives the impression that language evolves by leaps and bounds. Indeed, most parents feel that their children go from gestures to words in a matter of weeks. Then, after a period of relatively slow progress, two-word utterances appear, and suddenly the child explodes with new expressions. Children learn to talk overnight, so it seems.

"TALKING" BEFORE SPEECH

We have already seen that even newborns are disposed toward listening to speech. They are maximally attentive to sounds in the range of the human voice, to sound patterns and rhythms that characterize meaningful speech, and to the differences between sounds.

Early sounds. Babies utter more sounds than are in a single language. Thirty years ago at the State University of Iowa, Drs. O. C. Irwin and H. P. Chen studied these speechlike sounds in 40 infants during the first ten days of life. These scientists found that the infants produced vowel sounds more frequently than consonants. Every baby said *a* (as in *bat*); but *i* (as in *bite*), *e* (as in *bet*), and *u* (as in *but*) were also heard. The aspirate *h* (as in *house*) was the most frequently heard consonant, along with *w* and *k*. By four to six months of life, infants said most of the vowel sounds and about half the consonants, and by one year of age they produced, at one time or another, nearly all the sounds used in all the known languages of the world.

Regardless of the language of the parent, infants seem to speak sounds in a highly ordered sequence. That is, the first consonant sounds are formed in the back of the mouth, such as the aspirate *h* (*house*). Then infants tend to say *t* and *p*, which are produced farther forward in the mouth. Importantly, however, the progression is just the reverse for vowels. The sounds *i* and *e*, produced near the front of the mouth, are heard before *o*, which is generated farther back in the mouth. Since children of all nationalities, as well as deaf children who cannot hear a language spoken to them, go through nearly the same sequence during the first six months of life, it would appear that this progression is relatively inborn.

Babbling. Some time between four and six months of life, most infants emit a simple consonant-vowel syllable that they repeat in rapid succession, such as *bababa-ba*. No one knows why infants babble, but almost every child does it, even deaf children who cannot hear their parents speak and cannot hear themselves utter the sounds very well. However, sound production in deaf children begins to change at approximately six months of life, when it appears that hearing the sounds produced by oneself and others becomes important. Some researchers think that babbling helps to develop the muscles of the sound-producing apparatus: the infant comes to associate certain movements of the throat, tongue, and lips with certain sounds, and such "practicing" contributes to later speech production.

Between seven and ten months infants acquire patterns of intonation, and their babbling can become quite expressive. Most languages are spoken with a slight fall in frequency near the end of a sentence. On the other hand, questions are asked with a rise in pitch near the end. Embellished with such patterns of intonation, the babbling of a nine-month-old infant can sound almost like an adult speaking a foreign language. It can be so realistic that some parents become thoroughly convinced that their infants are talking to them, even to the point where they understand what the child is saying.

No one knows for sure just how or why children begin to speak different consonant-vowel combinations that sound like, and sometimes are, words. However, the Russian linguist, Roman Jakobson, has offered an intriguing theory. He suggests that infants adopt a strategy of first uttering two of the most opposite sounds in the language, and then producing the most contrasting sounds within each of those two categories, and so on. For example, two quite distinct sounds are *p* and *a* (as in *pen* and as in *bat*). *P* is a consonant that is formed at the front of the mouth and uses almost no vocal-cord action. In contrast, *a* is a vowel formed at the back of the mouth and requires considerable vocal-cord activity. The infant then combines *p* and *a* into *pa* and babbles that syllable as *papa*, which is often one of the first words infants say.

Development proceeds when infants work on two very opposite sounds within the same category as one of the two initial sounds. Typically these new sounds are consonants. Suppose the child uttered the consonant *p* as one of the first sounds, produced with the lips at the front of the mouth and using little or no vocal-cord activity. Another consonant in this same category, but opposite to *p*, is *m*, which is also made with the lips but involves a lot of vocal-cord activity. Thus, for infants who started with *p*, the next consonant they might add could be *m*. It is a short step to combining *m* with *a* to produce *ma* and *mama*. One wonders if the words for father and mother, which are quite similar from one language to the next, did not originate because infants are disposed to making such sounds as their first syllabic combinations or words. Not every infant begins speech with *pa* or *ma*, but Jakobson would argue that most begin with two extremely different sounds and then proceed to work on opposite sounds within each category.

First Words

The average child says a word for the first time at roughly one year of age, although perfectly normal children may not do so until as late as eighteen months. While language at this age is produced literally one word at a time, these single words seem to represent entire thoughts or sentences. A child may only utter the word *ball*, but depending upon the context, gestures, and intonation, this may mean "Give me the ball," "Is that a ball," or "Look at the ball." Actually a great deal of adult speech is also based not on the grammar and meaning of actual words, but on context. Adults are often surprised at how much they seem to "understand" a foreign language they do not speak, simply by paying attention to such cues. So too with toddlers.

Toddlers do not say just any words that come to mind. These one-word sentences represent a comment on an action or an expression of emotion. First words often communicate the child's approval, positive feeling, excitement, negative feeling, disapproval, or unhappiness. In addition, one-word sentences often comment on one of the child's own actions. While playing with a toy car that goes racing across the room, a child may say "bruumm," "go," or "bye-bye."

First words, especially nouns, are often applied to a host of objects, including many that adults would not refer to by that name. Most parents experience their child calling another adult "mama" or "papa." Such overextensions are done with a certain logic. That is, toddlers may call a wolf or a badger in a zoo a "doggie," but not a snake or a penguin. Typically, words are applied to new objects that have the same general shape and size as the object for which the word was learned originally.

First Sentences

Toddlers stay in the one-word phase for almost a year. Although some of the single words children utter are actually two words ("all gone"), the combining of two independent words into a meaningful new two-word utterance does not usually occur until sometime between eighteen and twenty-four months.

Why does it take so long for the child to be able to use two words at a time? No one knows for sure, but one guess is that the child must first have the ability to relate two things symbolically. As we have seen, this capability emerges between eighteen and twenty-four months. For a child to say "allgone milk" the youngster must not only know what "milk" and "allgone" represent, but these two symbols must be held in mind simultaneously and a connection made between them. Some psychologists believe that children are not able to use this combination until near the end of the second year.

There is more similarity from one youngster to the next in what two-year-olds talk about than the actual words they use. Perhaps the most obvious topic of conversation for children of this age is simply the *name* of things in the environment. The tendency for naming things starts during the one-word phase and continues when several-word utterances are possible. Children can wander into the kitchen and begin naming every object in sight—"cup," "milk," "cookie." And when they do this, they are not interested in simply talking to themselves—they want their parents to respond in some way, especially by looking at them and agreeing, "Yes, that's your cup." While this drives many parents to distraction, it is a very reasonable thing for the child to do.

Language is basically a social behavior, the purpose of which is to communicate information or influence the behavior of others. In some sense, language is not worth learning unless it "works," and children at this age spend considerable time exploring what influence words have on people. When they announce "see doggie," they expect an adult to look—that's what language is for.

Another topic of two-year-old conversation is the *location* of objects. Often youngsters will say "dere milk" or "here cup." They also request that certain actions be repeated. A favorite expression is "do 'ghen," which was one child's way to get someone to continue tickling.

Two-word utterances are sometimes used to express the *nonexistence* of objects, and the favorite here appears to be "allgone milk" to indicate that a cup of milk has been finished. *Negatives* are also employed, and some children walk around telling their parents what every household item is not—"not cat . . . dat doggie."

Toddlers also communicate *possession* in simple terms, such as "daddy chair." They ask *questions* by stating declarative sentences with rising intonation or by combining a question word ("where") with a noun ("where doggie?").

Some time later in the two-word phase, infants will combine *agent, action, and object.* At first, infants seem to understand that when Dad throws a ball there is an agent ("dada"), an action ("throw"), and an object ("ball"), but they can only say two of these at a time, such as "dada throw," "throw ball," or "dada ball." Later they will get them all together in "dada throw ball."

The point here is that a child's language is acquired in an orderly manner, and although the sounds and words will differ from child to child and from culture to culture, the general outline of development, strategy, and content of early speech seems quite similar from child to child and across nationalities.

Chapter Eight
Social Development

THERE IS MUCH to celebrate in the second year. Most children learn to walk quite well. They begin to talk, develop the rudiments of symbolic thinking, understand that they can influence the behavior of other people, and form the beginnings of a concept of self. Collectively, these advances mean that children become more active social persons, responding to others and requiring others to respond to them.

Steps Toward Personality

While infants in the first year of life have definite personalities, in the second year they are far more capable of putting that personality to work. There was once just a new person in the house, but now there is a new personality to reckon with—to accommodate, to help adjust to family conventions, to discipline, to enjoy. A toddler's mental and social abilities increase through a series of stages or phases. Arnold Gesell observed many babies and interviewed numerous parents regarding their children's social behavior. Although his research was performed several decades ago, no one has made such a thorough study since then.

Gesell found that "good" phases alternated with "bad" ones. Every few months, toddlers seemed to have it all together. Their parents would describe them as a source of happiness. Then everything would fall apart—the youngsters would be "out of bounds," and some would become uncontrollable and frustrating. Of course, not every child swung to such extremes, but many seemed to jump from easy to difficult phases and back again.

The one-year-old. The excitement that surrounds an infant's beginning to talk and walk is a joy to all, and the infant's ability to imitate adult actions gives parents the impression that a real person has joined the family. One-year-olds frequently love an audience, something they may have learned as a result of enthusiasm for their first words and first steps. Some youngsters are even "disciplined" at this age and will obey a parental no no. Basically, the months surrounding an infant's first birthday are a time when several skills have recently emerged (standing, walking, imitation, first words), and it seems as if infants merely want to exercise these new capabilities for an approving audience.

Fourteen to twenty months. But all good things come to an end—exercising skills becomes old. Toddlers now want to apply their abilities to new purposes. Youngsters no longer walk just to walk; they walk to go to a certain place and to do a particular thing. The infant is now much more capable of discovering new bits of information about objects around the house, because of an increase both in the physical ability to walk and in the mental ability to understand cause-and-effect relationships between objects. Toddlers of this age are great experimenters—manipulating, dropping, throwing, squeezing, and rattling everything they can get their hands on.

Their examination of objects appears very deliberate, even methodical. They seem so engrossed in applying their newfound ability to understand the world that they are oblivious to attempts to curb their adventuresomeness. Not only does this represent an affront to some parents' perception of their own authority, but it means that infants are more likely to get into dangerous situations (say, with stoves, electric sockets, scissors). They are simply unrestrained in their effort to see what this new world is about.

Twenty-one to twenty-five months. This is often described as a period of calm. Toddlers have seen most common household objects, which no longer are so fascinating. They are a little less preoccupied with getting into everything, often pay more attention to their parents, and can be loving and affectionate.

Symbolic skills emerge at this time, although they do not dominate the day-to-day social behavior of toddlers until a little later. These new mental abilities help toddlers not to become so upset when their parents leave or when strangers enter the room (unless crying has become a way to control parents). Presumably, youngsters have learned what to do in such circumstances. They have also discovered that their parents, who may be absent at the moment, nevertheless do exist and will return.

New symbolic skills also mean that infants are now capable of understanding that they exist as entities in the environment. This has been demonstrated in a clever experiment. Children of this age whose noses were reddened with rouge were placed in front of a large mirror. They were much more likely to touch their own noses as a means of exploring the red color than to touch the mirror, as did younger infants. Presumably, they knew that a mirror reflects their own images and actions and is not only an object in itself to be explored. Of course, a person's self-concept grows over many years, but this seems to be the beginning.

Beyond twenty-five months. Although this may be a period of relative calm for many children, it precedes what is sometimes one of the most difficult periods in childrearing—what Gesell called the "terrible twos." When toddlers come to understand more fully that they are independent, dynamic forces in their own environments, they begin to explore their potential for influencing other people, especially parents. From a toddler's perspective, the major purpose is to explore what actions other people will take in response to one or another of their own actions. From a parent's standpoint, such "manipulating" may be perceived as defiance and disobedience. Consequently, it is quite understandable for parents to try to discipline their toddler. But to the infant, the discipline can also be something to be explored—"What do I have to do to get Mom to say no or to get slapped on the hand?" Many toddlers are apparently willing to endure punishment while they explore these social cause-and-effect relationships.

Life with a two-and-a-half-year-old can be quite frustrating. A well-intentioned mother may ask her little boy whether he wants cornflakes or bran for breakfast. Cornflakes is the request. After the milk is poured, he changes his mind and wants bran. Moreover, he behaves as if he had wanted bran all along, and he may become very upset at his mother's attempt to explain and reason with him. But reasonable behavior is not the youngster's goal; getting his mother to do something—anything—is the task. And the more the mother gets upset, the more influence he has. If she decides to ignore the request for bran and leaves the cornflakes as originally ordered, he screams or throws a tantrum. If she now capitulates, gives the cornflakes to the dog, and serves up a spanking new bowl of bran, the boy has learned that a good screaming tantrum is a very effective way to control his mother and get what he wants.

On some occasions, toddlers are more obvious in communicating that the purpose of their defiance is to get the parent to do something. For example, children may deliberately reach for forbidden objects (say a TV or kitchen knife), but at the same time they will watch their parents to see what the reactions will be. The children probably know that what they are doing is against the rules, and they may not even be interested in obtaining the forbidden item. But they are interested to see what their parents will do. Most children are not being malicious or deliberately defiant. They are simply exploring social relationships and responses in the same way they explore a fascinating toy. They must learn these lessons, and such social experimentation probably helps them do so.

Parents should be sensitive to the fact that sometimes their attempt at discipline is not punishing at all but is actually rewarding to the child—"What better way to get Dad to drop everything and run right over to me than to sprinkle salt all over the carpet?" If the child is in no apparent danger, if the house will not be destroyed, and if the parents perceive that they, not the salt shaker, are the real objects of interest, parents can try ignoring the child. The logic is that if the child wants to see the parent run and get angry, then not running or not getting angry will deny the child the desired response. Afterward, parents might offer a two-sentence explanation on why we do not salt the carpet and proclaim that people who make messes must clean them up. Then parents might permit the child to organize the vacuuming to be done by both parent and child, which is a more appropriate way for the child to influence the behavior of the parent.

Regardless of one's approach, these can be trying times for parents, and one can only take heart that such behavior happens often enough to be regarded as "normal," and it usually subsides—only to reappear occasionally.

PLAY

The play behavior of toddlers becomes considerably more childlike, deliberate, and imaginative during the second and especially third year of life. No one knows exactly why children play. It has been observed that play is an activity of the "idle rich" among animal species. Animals who do not need to spend many hours searching for food, who are not constantly pursued by predators, and who are capable of adapting to a variety of different environments play more than other species. Perhaps it is not surprising, then, that nineteenth-century writers suggested that play was a relatively purposeless release of "surplus energy." But any parent knows that this is not always true. Two-year-olds will refuse to go to bed even when utterly exhausted, if they are given the opportunity to play instead.

Other reasons for play have been offered. Some scholars believe childhood play is the exercising of skills that would be valuable later in the child's life. Still others in the early 1900s thought that the playing child reenacts the interests and occupations of evolutionary predecessors. A child's climbing and swinging were viewed as repeating the actions of man's ape ancestors, and the water play of children was a vestige of our aquatic origins.

More recent thought assumes that play is not without purpose or benefit to the child. Psychoanalysts have long suggested that children in play act out fantasies that reduce tension created by unpleasant experiences. Actually there is very little scientific support for this notion. Instead it is widely acknowledged that most play is usually free of anxiety, and children perform a variety of imagined activities in their play, not just ones that have been associated with past unpleasantness.

Learning and social practice. Why do children play? Two ideas have reappeared over the decades of thought on this topic. The first is that the child learns something about objects and social relations. The second is that play provides a relatively safe, relaxed, free context to explore objects and social relationships that might otherwise be threatening.

Dr. Jane Lawick-Goodall observed that when chimpanzees play in trees they probably learn which branches will support their weights. Also, the young chimps explored how a reed may be used to extract termites from a hole, knowledge and skills they need to know later. Play, especially pretending, also allows children imaginatively to control and influence the environment in ways not possible in reality. "Cops and robbers," "house," "parent and baby," or "cars and trucks" all permit the child greater control and influence over the environment than children can attain in reality.

A study by Dr. Kathy Silva of Oxford University shows that children can learn something about objects simply by playing with them. Silva asked middle-class children from a day-care center to obtain a piece of chalk contained within a latched box. The problem was that the box was out of reach and could not be touched by either of two available sticks. However, the chalk could be obtained by clamping the sticks together, undoing the latch with the extended stick, and raking out the chalk. Children were given different experiences before they were allowed to tackle the problem themselves. Some children watched an adult construct the tool and solve the problem. Others were allowed to play freely with the sticks in any way they chose, while still others were given instruction by an adult on how to put the sticks together and solve the problem. Finally, a fourth group was not instructed at all or given any play time with the materials before being asked to solve the problem. The results indicated that simply playing with the sticks without any special instruction was just as effective in helping the children solve the problem as was watching an adult accomplish the feat. Both these experiences were more effective than having an adult directly train the children.

Why was direct training *less* effective? Perhaps children don't want to be told what to do—they want to decide themselves. For example, other research suggests that when adults tell children how to use objects and how to play, the children are less interested in exploring and playing with those objects than if adults do not make any suggestions. Children in the second and certainly third years of life have just learned how to influence objects and people in a variety of new ways. Moreover, it is a fact of development that infants and toddlers tend to exercise, almost *ad nauseam,* newly developed skills. Therefore, parents and nursery teachers might want to ensure that there are places and times when children are allowed to play safely with minimum adult interference. This is the fundamental principle that Maria Montessori championed in her approach to early education.

Getting Along with Peers

Until a child is able to crawl or walk, the ability to relate to other infants of the same age is severely limited. However, from the beginning of the second year, most children are sufficiently mobile so that they can initiate and retreat from social relations with children of their own age.

From adults to peers. The first social relations between infants and their parents consist primarily of looking at one another. In adult-infant relationships the adult is often very cooperative and holds the infant nearby while looking into the infant's eyes. This permits the infant to gaze at or away from the parent, who is nevertheless always present for substantial periods of time. Thus the infant can exert a certain measure of control over the social situation because the parent is more or less willing to be a partner.

But when two infants are together, they do not sit still and look into each other's eyes, despite the apparent fascination with which one infant studies another. Toddlers are interested in exploring each other, but curiosity has its limits, especially when there is considerable uncertainty over what the object of exploration (the other infant) will do in this situation. The infant is more experienced with manipulating and exploring toys; they are a little more predictable, a little safer than another child.

Inevitably, a toy that interests one toddler will also interest another. The two toddlers may both look at the object, especially if the toy continues to rock or make noise after being jostled or thrown. But then both toddlers may reach for the toy, and for twelve-to-fifteen month infants, possession is ten tenths of the law of social relations. Because most toddlers are still oriented toward objects, it is not surprising that tussles over toys punctuate their play, especially when only one toy of each kind is available for members of the group. Of course, toddlers are fairly good at sizing up the social power of their colleagues, and many will quickly, but unhappily, relinquish a toy to a more aggressive partner.

Dr. Edward Mueller at Boston University has described the way in which children progress toward more mature relations with their peers. Mueller's observations show that the first contact between young toddlers usually focuses around objects and possible conflicts over possessing them. Soon, however, youngsters may begin to take turns with a toy. At first this is fortuitous—one child plays with an attractive object, and when it is discarded for a new toy, the other child picks it up. Later, turn taking will be more deliberate.

Sometimes a rudimentary form of social influencing occurs in the context of "give and take." Toddlers who see themselves as being socially more aggressive often simply take objects from other children. But toddlers who see themselves as equal to their partner may adopt the strategy of giving a toy to their peer. It is safer than taking, and in some sense it influences the behavior of the other child just as effectively.

Influencing at a distance. Eventually more mature social relations must be conducted at a distance. When adults engage in social activities, they interact through conversation. Toddlers are not as facile in their language, and in the absence of these skills they have learned to influence objects and people in their environment primarily by pushing and pulling. How then do they learn to influence another child without touching?

One way this may occur is through mutual imitation. That is, one child discovers an interesting thing to do with a toy while the other child watches. Then the observer picks up the toy and imitates the actions of the first child. The experience of seeing oneself imitated by another helps the toddler come to the tacit realization of having influenced another person. The research of Mueller and many other scientists indicates that the play of young toddlers contains frequent episodes of mutual imitation, including the imitation of actions with an object, "talking" to one another, and playing "peek-a-boo" or "follow-the-leader." This is a fundamental social lesson to be learned in the second and third years of life, since almost all mature social relations consist of influencing others at a distance, usually through language.

The next step is for the child to explore and exercise this newfound skill. Thus toddlers may imitate each other over and over again until even they find it silly. Then a new twist is introduced. Now when one child imitates another, the initiator may change the behavior to see if the partner will follow suit. One child may roll a ball to knock over some bowling pins, but the other varies the game by kicking the remaining pins over. Then the two bowlers may set the pins up again and send a doll and a truck crashing into the pins. Up to this point, toddlers have usually stumbled into social exchanges—one youngster happens to be doing something interesting with an object when a peer takes notice and joins in. But now in the second year of life, when symbolic mental abilities have arrived, children are able to plan social encounters. One child may suddenly get up, retrieve the bowling ball, and sail it into the pins, all the while looking at the play partner to see what social impact this action will have. Bowling is not primarily intended to knock the pins down; it is intended to elicit a response from the peer. At this point, toddlers are well on their way to creative social relations with other children.

Fighting. Just because progress toward mature social relations is underway does not rule out fighting. Fortunately, most squabbles between toddlers are not what they seem. While struggles over toys can be serious and the loser may emerge in tears, the "aggressor" is not usually angry or intent on hurting the other child. These conflicts may arise for one of two major reasons. First, two children want the same toy, and most young toddlers simply don't know—and perhaps are too young to learn—another way of obtaining the toy. In this case, caregivers probably need to break up the fight, and provide two toys or help the second child to find another toy until the desired object is free. Two-year-olds do not share very well, nor do they have a sense of fair play.

The second reason for toddler fighting looks more serious. One child may appear to be a bully. In one of my own studies on the play behavior of two-year-olds, one boy suddenly stood up from playing with a truck, walked over to his peer, and punched him squarely in the nose. And he did it utterly poker-faced and without provocation. Then he stepped back and watched the other boy cry, again without much expression. After a moment, both children returned to separate play. The child who started the hitting was big, and we wondered if he would be so aggressive if he were paired with an equally large and scrappy youngster. We forewarned both sets of parents before the play session began that fighting might occur. Our "aggressive" boy did the same thing—he just popped the other fellow in the face.

After we watched the television recordings of these

episodes and interviewed the mother of this boy, a picture of the child emerged that helped us understand the hitting behavior a little better. First, the child did not seem to hit out of anger. Sometimes he even offered a toy as if to try to play with the other child. Second, he never talked to the other child or even to his own mother. Third, while this youngster and his mother were waiting in the lobby for the play session to begin, we noticed that the boy was not allowed to do anything for himself. If he looked over at magazines on the table, his mother would anticipate him, fetch one, and turn the pages for him. Finally, the mother told us that the little boy and his father play-wrestled almost every night.

We concluded that the child simply had not learned how to influence adults or peers except by physical means—and he was quite successful at that method. It was as if he thought, "This is the way you play with other children." Indeed, we found other youngsters, who were ordinarily not prone to hitting, resort to it if there appeared to be no other way to influence the other child. And fighting will produce a response in the other child just about every time.

Without help and encouragement, children who have not learned socially acceptable ways to influence other children may become more aggressive. Dr. Gerald Patterson of the University of Oregon found that children disposed to physical means of social influencing increased this kind of behavior during the first weeks of nursery school because it worked. Their "victims" yielded toys and generally were fearful of them. Because it is difficult to prevent such aggressive behavior from achieving its goal—getting a response from the other child—these youngsters need guidance to learn that other methods can accomplish the same purpose.

Alternative Day Care

Parents obviously play a large role in fostering appropriate social behavior in their young children. But can the parent's role be shared effectively with other caregivers?

There was a time when a mother's role was in the home, and psychological theory dictated that infants needed their own biological, full-time mother for adequate psychological development. These days appear to be over. In the United States alone, more than half of the nation's mothers are employed outside the home. As a result, today's parents are concerned with selecting alternative care for their children. Are these youngsters being harmed or short-changed by these experiences?

Mental development. Dr. Henry Ricciuti of Cornell University has recently surveyed the research on infant day care for the U.S. Department of Health, Education, and Welfare. He concludes that there is generally no evidence that even prolonged experience in infant day care beginning as early as the first year of life has any adverse effects on intellectual development *if the care provided is of high quality.* Almost no research has been done on day care of low quality, and it is possible that such experiences could retard intellectual and social development.

Excellent day care that stresses a structured attempt to improve mental development can have positive effects for children. Mental performance may improve if the day-care program provides experiences that supplement those of the child's home, although such gains do not appear until about two years of age, the advent of symbolic thinking. But most children come from homes that provide sufficiently good intellectual experiences and they will not show gains in intelligence as a result of day-care experiences. Even if increases do occur, they are not likely to endure into childhood unless the program of enrichment continues.

Social development. Are children enrolled in day care less attached to their parents? In his survey Ricciuti concludes that no evidence supports the view that extended experience in day care beginning in the first two years of life has a disruptive influence on the affectional relationships between infant and parent. However, he hastens to add that the research is not very complete and that only professionally designed programs of high quality have been examined.

Infants enrolled in day care sometimes adapt more easily and comfortably to unfamiliar social situations in the absence of the mother, but it is not clear whether this is good, bad, or inconsequential. We are not yet able to determine an answer.

WHAT IS THE BEST CARE?

Ricciuti's conclusion is that day care of high quality does not seem to harm youngsters and, if it supplements their home experiences, it may be intellectually beneficial. He suggests that parents look for a day-care setting that comes close to what they consider a good, natural home environment. Specifically, parents can check to see that the physical surroundings provide enough safe space for children to play inside and outside; a clean and well-maintained kitchen and bathroom; facilities for the care of sick children or for handling emergencies; and adequate play equipment (books and art supplies).

While a safe, cheerful physical facility is important, it is not sufficient. The number and personal style of caregivers is crucial. For children under two months of age, there should be one caregiver for every two children, though this ratio changes as the children become older. For example, one adult to every five two- or three-year-olds is probably quite adequate. While ratios of one-to-eight or one-to-ten are to be avoided, even one adult for every one or two children does not guarantee a superior program, and new evidence indicates that the size of the group of children is more important that the sheer number of caregivers.

The caregivers should have goals for the growth and development of children that are consistent with those of the parent. Most parents would want the caregivers to be affectionate and responsive; to interact with infants in ways that foster a sense of basic trust and confidence in adults; to create enjoyable opportunities for learning, play, and social interactions; and to deal sensitively with the individual needs of the child.

A parent will probably want to feel that the caregivers really seem to like children, have a calm personality and a sense of humor, listen when children talk, and control the group with kind but firm discipline. Are children allowed to play freely and do things for themselves? Are they having a good time? Are the children learning something? Often, highly structured "curricula" for the stimulation and education of young children are impressive, but an informal approach in which the "teachers" take advantage of momentary situations to show the child something may be equally or more effective.

Finally, parents might inquire about the extent to which they will be involved in their children's day-care experience. Are parents encouraged to help their children adapt to their new environment, and will the caregivers instill the same values and use the same disciplinary practices that the parent would invoke were the child at home?

Ideally parents should observe several alternative centers or family-care homes before making a selection, and once a tentative choice has been made, the parent and child should visit the facility together. If, after several weeks of attendance, the child cries when taken to the center or home, becomes increasingly upset when the parent leaves, or exhibits a growing number of nervous symptoms (thumb sucking, bed wetting, hair pulling, listlessness, refusal to eat, fear of going to sleep), perhaps the parent should consider a change.

Are Parents Necessary?

It has become apparent that feeding, diapering, and other caretaking duties are not the basis of attachment and love. Whereas it once was thought that love grew out of the feeding situation, we now know this is not the case. Infants develop attachments with their fathers, who typically do not feed or may not even spend a great deal of time with them. Children also develop attachments with their grandparents, who may not live in the same home or town.

Attachment appears to be based not on the amount of time spent with children but on how that time is spent. A sensitive, responsive, relationship between parent and infant is especially important, one in which parents make their responses contingent to their infant's actions and respect their infant's desire to influence and control the social situation. This may take only a few minutes a day, as in the case of the father who played bumpty-bump with his daughter. But it does require some concentrated, undivided attention, and a few minutes of "infant-only" time may be worth hours of the casual time spent with the baby nearby. Special games may take place at any time, during and after feeding or changing, when the father gets home, or just when baby or parents feel like it. The most important sign that such games are going well is that parents and infant are having a good time.

Rudolph Schaffer sums it up this way:

> Do babies need mothers? Yes—if it means that they need to be involved in a love relationship, that satisfaction of their physical wants alone is not enough. No—if it means that mother must be the one who gave birth, that no other person can take her place. No again—if we take mothering to involve an exclusive care relationship that must encapsulate the child's total social and emotional life; on the contrary, there are many arguments for allowing the child to widen his interpersonal horizon from the beginning and for not discouraging other attachments. And finally yes—if we mean that a limited range of familiar people should provide consistent care throughout the years of childhood. (*Mothering* [Cambridge: Harvard University Press, 1977], p. 106.)

Fathers. Dr. Michael Lamb of the University of Michigan points out that historically fathers have been considered relatively unimportant and uninterested in infant rearing, and perhaps even incapable. The father was supposed to provide occasional babysitting services and emotional support to the mother who was the primary, if not the only, psychological caregiver.

While it is true that some men spend very little time with their infants (one study reported fathers talked to their young infants only 37 seconds per day) and many abhor changing messy diapers, these attitudes are not as widespread as some people think. Research shows that the birth of a child has a strong emotional impact on most fathers, and approximately half of the mothers interviewed in one study said their husbands would "do anything for their infants." Moreover, when fathers are observed in the newborn nursery in the absence of the mother, they immediately perform both maternal and paternal caretaking duties quite naturally and competently. Babies in the first year will choose to go to their fathers just as often, and sometimes even more frequently, as to their mothers, although under stress they prefer their mothers.

Most people feel that fathers help their sons grow up to be "a man," but fathers also contribute to a daughter's sex-role development. Prior to their child's first birthday, fathers interact in much the same way with both sons and daughters. Thereafter, however, they spend almost twice as much time with their sons while the mother interacts equivalently with her toddlers regardless of sex. Subsequently, sons begin to show a greater preference for their fathers. Other research on sexual reassignment and father absence suggests that the father plays a vital part during the first two years in sex-role development, although his influence may not be seen until the child is much older. Moreover, masculine boys and feminine girls are *not* the offspring of authoritarian, stereotypic "masculine" fathers. Rather, warm, nurturant fathers who form a close loving relationship with their children are the ones who have appropriately masculine sons and feminine daughters.

Finally, fathers also probably influence their infant's mental development. Fathers and mothers play differently with their toddlers. Mothers tend to engage in conventional games using toys while fathers are more unpredictable and physically stimulating in their play. In addition, mothers pick up and hold their infants primarily for caregiving purposes and to restrict explorations, while fathers hold their infants to play with them or because the baby just wants to be held. It is known from research with older children that fathers teach their offspring, especially their sons, to want to tackle problems they encounter with confidence. Perhaps the creative, vigorous style of a father's play is the beginning of that lesson. In any case, fathers are not disinterested, incompetent, or unimportant.

Our notions of motherhood and fatherhood are changing. Care and feeding are necessary tasks, but they are not the materials of which love between parent and infant is made. Rather, infants and parents become attached to one another when they play, when one responds to the other in appropriate and consistent ways, when one allows the other to lead as well as follow, and when a parent takes time to care, to guide, and to share. But it is not so much the amount of time spent with the infant; it is the nature of what happens during this time that is important in causing love between parent and child, fostering the child's development, and creating the joy and fulfillment that can accompany family life.

Index

Abuse of infants, 68-69
Activity, 103-104
Acuity, newborn's visual, 51-53
Ahrens, R., 113
Ainsworth, M., 39, 117
Ambrose, A., 111
Arena, J. M., 35-36
Attachment: newborn's preparation for, 49-61; infant's recognition of parent, 51-52, 54, 57-60, 88-89, 91-92; as instinct, 61-69; parent's response to baby, 61-69; when mothers feel it for newborn, 68; role of communicating and influencing between parent and newborn, 69-74; role of mutual gazing, 70; role of early contact and bonding, 70-74; and personality in the first year, 102-128; and responsive play, 116-125
Audition: newborn's capability, 55-58; newborn's response to human speech, 55-58

Babbling, 141-142
Babyishness, 61-66
Bayley, scales of infant development, 24
Bell, S. M., 39, 117
Birch, H., 103-107
Birth weight, size of mother, 18-19
Bonding, 70-74
Bowlby, J., 122

Brackbill, Y., 111
Breastfeeding, 34-37
Bronowski, J., 137
Bruner, J., 93-95

Caldwell, B., 33
Chen, H. P., 140
Chess, S., 103-107
Circumcision, 39-40
Clarke, A. D. B., 10
Clarke, A. M., 10
Colic, 110
Communication: crying, 108-112; mutual gazing, 108; smiling, 112-114; between parent and infant, 114-116; special faces, 114-115; lack between parent and infant, 119-124
Condon, W., 57
Crying, 38-39, 108-112

Davis, K., 9-10
Day care, 158-161
DDT, in breast milk and formulas, 35
Defiance, in two-year-olds, 148-150
Dement, W. C., 43
Dennis, W., 25
Deprivation, 8-10, 33-34
Development: preformationism, 3-5; predeterminism, 5-6; heredity and environment, 6-11; effects of early experience, 7-11

Douglas, J., 122
Dreaming, 42-44
Dunn, J., 109

Early contact, 70-74
Early experience: effects on development, 7-11; case of Isabelle, 8-10; recovery from deprivation, 8-10; case of Monica, 33-34
Eibl-Eibesfeldt, I., 61
Eimas, P., 56
Eisenberg, R., 55
Engen, T., 58
Eriksen, E., 33
Exercise, 26
Experience. See Early experience; Stimulation
Eye-to-eye contact, 70-74

Faces, newborn's visual scanning, 54
Fagan, J., 92
Fathers, special role, 162-164
Feeding: obesity, 22-23; solids, 22-23; vitamins, 23; temperature regulation, 30; role of sucking, 32-33; case of Monica, 33-34; psychological importance, 33-34; breast vs. bottle, 34-37; psychological benefits, 36; four-hour schedule, 37-38; schedule or self-demand, 37-38; spoiling baby, 38-39; thumbsucking and pacifiers, 39-41
Fels Research Institute, 8, 13, 79
Fighting, 156-157
Fontanels, 68
Formulas vs. breastfeeding, 34-37
Freud, S., 7-8
Friedman, S., 83

Gesell, A., 5-6, 146-150
Grobstein, R., 110
Growth: physical, 12-26; charts, 13-19; catch-up after illness, 17-18; predicting adult size, 17-19; national differences, 20; prematurity, 20-21; role of diet, 20; role of hormones, 20; obesity, 22-23; breast vs. formula, 35
Gustation. See Taste

Haith, M., 53
Hearing. See Audition
Heredity: in intelligence, 6-11, 79-81; myths about 7; influence on physical growth, 19-20
Hindley, C. B., 25
Hippocrates, 3-4
Homunculus, 4
Hormones, role in physical growth, 20
Hutt, J., 55

Ik, 69
Illingworth, R., 110
Imitation, 89-91, 134-135, 155-156
Immunizations, in breast milk, 34
Intelligence: changes over age, 8; predictions to adult IQ, 8; case of Isabelle, 8-10; recovery from deprivation, 8-10; growth of, 77-101; nature of, 77-83, 87-88; heritability, 79-81; predicting IQ from infant tests, 81; role of stimulation, 81-83; functions, 87-88; stages, 88-100, 132-137; language development, 131-145; effects of day care, 158-159
IQ. See Intelligence
Irritability, 104
Irwin, O. C., 140
Isabelle, case of, 8-10

Jakobson, R., 141
James, W., 49
Jumping, age of onset, 24

Kaye, H., 58
Kaye, K., 85
Kennell, J., 70-74
Kessen, W., 53
Klaus, M., 70-74
Korner, A., 110

Lamb, M., 162
Language: case of Isabelle, 8-10; first words, 11, 135-136, 142-143; labeling objects, 99-100; preverbal communication, 108-124; two-word sentences, 136-137, 143-144; vocabulary development, 139-140; early sounds, 140-141; semantic content, 144-145
Lanugo, 67
Lawick-Goodall, J., 151
Learned helplessness, 120-121
Learning: newborn's capability, 83-87; in fetus, 84; to suck, 84-85; guidelines for teaching, 85-87
Leiderman, H., 70, 73
Lipsitt, L., 58, 111
Locke, J., 102
Lorenz, K., 61
Love. See Attachment

Macfarlane, A., 58, 68
Mason, M., 9-10
Mead, M., 69
Meltzoff, A., 89
Memory, 92, 99-100
Mendel, G., 6
Milk, breast and formula, 34-36
Millar, S., 85-86
Mills, M., 57
Monica, case of, 33-34
Montessori, M., 153
Moore, M. K., 89
Moro reflex, 45-46
Moss, H., 68
Motor development: milestones in, 23-25; effect of experience and training, 25-26
Movement, newborn's accompaniment to human speech, 57-58
Mueller, E., 154
Mundugumoro, 69
Mutual gazing, 115-116
Muzil, J. N., 43

National Center for Health Statistics, 13
Newborn: capabilities, 29-48; appearance, 66-68
Nilsson, L., 41
Nutrition: role in physical growth, 20; obesity, 22-23; breast vs. formula, 34-36. See also Feeding

Obesity, 22-23
Object permanency, 95-100, 132-134
Objects, infants' knowledge about, 91, 95-99, 132-134
Olfaction. See Smell
Orwell, G., 55

Pacifiers, 39-41
Parent: infant's recognition, 88-89, 91-92, 110; the sensitive, 117-125; lack of responsiveness, 120-121; separations from, 121-123; need for, 161-162
Patterson, G., 157
Personality: early temperaments and styles, 103-107; stages in second year, 147-150
Piaget, J., 98, 100
Play: responsive social, 116-125; theories of, 150-153; with peers, 153-157
Predeterminism, 5-6
Preformationism, 3-5

Prematurity: 3, 20-21; future growth potential, 21; small for gestational age, 21; true prematures, 21
Prenatal development, 3, 18-19

Rapid eye movement (REM) sleep, 42-44
Reaching and grasping, 93-96
Reflexes: rooting, 41, 44-45; Moro, 45-46; standing and walking, 46-48
Ricciuti, H., 158-159
Richards, M., 109, 114
Robson, K., 68
Rocking, 110-111
Roffwarg, H. P., 43
Rooting reflex, 44-45
Rutter, M., 121

Salapatek, P., 53
Salisbury, D., 60
Sameroff, A., 84
Sander, L., 57, 117-118
Schaffer, H. R., 117, 122, 162
Schedules, feeding, 37-39
Seeing. *See* Vision
Self-concept, first sign, 148
Self-demand feeding, 37-39
Seligman, M., 121
Separation of infant from parent, 121-123, 125-128
Sitting, age of, 24
Silva, K., 152
Sleep: hours per night, 41-42; dreaming, 42-44
Small for gestational age, 21
Smell: newborn's capability, 58-60; newborn's recognition of mother, 58-59
Smiling, 112-114
Social development, 146-164
Social responsivity, 104-105

Solomon, R., 120
Sontag, L., 84
Spoiling, 39, 110
Standing: age of, 24; reflex, 46-48
Stayton, D. J., 117
Stern, D., 66, 114, 123-124
Stimulation: effects on intelligence, 7-11, 81-83; effects on motor development, 25-26. *See also* Early experience
Strangers, infant's fear of, 125-128
Sucking, 32-33; need to, 40; calming effect, 111-112
Swaddling, 111
Symbolic relations, 136-137; relation to social behavior, 148, 155

Taste, newborn's capability, 60-61
Temperament: activity, 103-104; irritability, 104; social responsivity, 104-105
Temperature, 29-31
Terrible twos, 148-150
Thoman, E., 110
Thomas, A., 103-107
Thumbsucking, 39-41
Toys, 100
Twins, 25

van Leeuwenhoek, A., 4
Vernix, 66
Vision: newborn's capability, 50-54; rules of looking, 53-54; newborn's scanning of faces, 54
Vitamins, 23

Walking, 11; age of, 24; national differences, 25; significance of age, 23-26; reflex, 46-48
Watson, J., 86, 118, 121
Watson, J. B., 102
Wolff, D. F., 5
Wolff, P., 111

Credits

4   Carnegie Institute.

5   J. Needham, *A History of Embryology* (New York: Abelard-Schuman, 1959). Originally published in N. Hartsoecker, *Essay de dioptrique* (Paris, 1694).

14–17   Data adapted from U.S. National Center for Health Statistics: NCHS Growth Charts, 1976, based on the Fels Research Institute Study.

18, 43, 113, 138   *Developmental Psychology Today,* 2nd ed. Copyright 1975 by Random House, Inc. Reprinted by permission of CRM Books, a division of Random House, Inc.

38   W. Kessen, M. M. Haith, and P. H. Salapatek, in *Carmichael's Manual of Child Psychology,* P. H. Mussen, ed. (New York: John Wiley and Sons, 1970). Adapted from C. A. Aldrich and E. S. Hewitt, *Journal of the American Medical Association,* 1947, *135,* 341.

43   Adapted from Roffwarg, Dement, and Fischer, in *Behavior in Infancy and Early Childhood,* Y. Brackbill and S. G. Thompson, eds. (New York: Free Press, 1967).

45–47   H. F. R. Prechtl and D. Beintema, *The Neurological Examination of the Full-Term Newborn Infant,* 2nd ed., Clinics in Developmental Medicine, no. 63 (London: Spastics International Medical Publications with Heinemann Medical Books; Philadelphia: Lippincott, 1977).

50   T. B. Brazelton, *Neonatal Behavioral Assessment Scale,* Clinics in Developmental Medicine, no. 50 (London: Spastics International Medical Publications with Heinemann Medical Books; Philadelphia: Lippincott, 1973).

52   Chris Maynard.

59   Ruth Silverman (Stock/Boston).

62   Wide World Photos and the Omaha *World-Herald* (26 November 1977).

63   Thomas McAvoy, *Life,* copyright 1955 by Time, Inc.

64 E. H. Hess, in *Carmichael's Manual of Child Psychology*, P. H. Mussen, ed. (New York: John Wiley and Sons, 1970). Adapted from K. Z. Lorenz, *Zeitschrift fur Tierpsychologie*, V (1943), 276.

65 C. M. Jackson, in W. J. Robbins, et al., eds., *Growth* (New Haven: Yale University Press, 1929), p. 118.

67 A. K. Tunstill, Department of Medical Illustration, Hallamshire Hospital, Sheffield, England.

72 John Hedgecoe, from *The Psychology of Childbirth* by Aidan Macfarlane (London: Open Books, 1977).

90 From the collection of T.G.R. Bower. In T.G.R. Bower, *The Perceptual World of the Child* (Cambridge, Mass.: Harvard University Press, 1977).

94 J. S. Bruner, *Processes of Cognitive Growth: Infancy* (Worcester, Mass: Clark University Press, 1968).

96-97 Monkmeyer Press Photo Service, New York.

101 Peter Vandermark (Stock/Boston).

110 Courtesy of John Lind, from V. Vuorenkoski, O. Wasz-Höckert, and E. Koivisto, "The Effect of Cry Stimulus on the Temperature of the Lactating Breast of Primipara. A Thermographic Study," *Experientia*, 1969, *25*, 1286.

125 Community Services Administration (formerly the Office of Economic Opportunity).

158 Julie O'Neil (Stock/Boston).

Drawings and graphs on pages 14–17, 18, 38, and 138 were adapted by Richard Spencer.